M

Modern Tagalog

Modern Tagalog

Grammatical Explanations and Exercises for Non-native Speakers

TERESITA V. RAMOS
RESTY M. CENA

University of Hawaii Press
Honolulu

Library of Congress Cataloging-in-Publication Data

Ramos, Teresita V.
  Modern Tagalog : grammatical explanations and exercises for non-
native speakers / Teresita V. Ramos, Resty M. Cena.
    p. cm.
  ISBN 0-8248-1332-4
  1. Tagalog language—Grammar.   2. Tagalog language—Phonology.
I. Cena, Resty M.   II. Title.
PL6053.R278   1990
499'.21182421—dc20   90-15577
                                                       CIP

Camera-ready copy for this book
was prepared by Resty M. Cena.

Contents

Chapter 3. The Verb: Aspect and Focus   47

Chapter 4. Simple Expansions of the Basic Sentence   63

Chapter 5. Some Changes in the Basic Sentence 81

Chapter 6. Complex Sentences: Conjoining 109

Chapter 7. More on Conjoining   139

Chapter 8. Complex Sentences: Embedding   153

Preface

The purpose of *Modern Tagalog: Grammatical Explanations and Exercises for Non-Native Speakers* is to provide advanced students of Tagalog as a foreign language with practice on points that range from phonology to syntax. While the emphasis of these exercises is on written work, many of them may be used for oral drill as well.

The exercises are arranged systematically for ease of location. They progress from the less difficult to the more difficult. Explanations are kept to a minimum.

Chapter 1 deals with the description of Tagalog sounds, with drills that focus on the sounds difficult for native English speakers. This is followed by a section on sound changes and cases of stress shift. A short exercise on pitch and intonation concludes this chapter.

Chapter 2 discusses three general classes of simple sentences: sentences with a subject, subjectless sentences, and existential sentences.

Chapter 3 focuses on the verb and its two important features: aspect and focus. Aspect refers to the expression of duration in the verb, and focus to the expression in the verb of the role of the subject or primary participant in the action.

Chapter 4 describes how the basic sentence is expanded in three simple ways: identify other participants in the event; modify the event, the participants, or the modifiers; and compound the event, the participants, or the modifiers.

Chapter 5 begins with some structural changes in the basic sentence such as inverted sentences, negative sentences, questions, commands, requests, and exhortations. Then come more functions of the verbs such as aptative/abilitative and social-participative functions. The chapter ends with the use and meaning of enclitics.

Chapters 6, 7, and 8 describe complex sentences which are combinations of two or more simple sentences. Chapters 6 and 7 focus on *conjoining*, the joining of two sentences one after the other. The last chapter (8) focuses on *embedding* one sentence inside another.

The sequence of practice moves from simple to complex structures. Mastery of these structures is especially important for writing since they provide grammatical shapes for the expression of predications and thus relate grammar to meaning. At the end of each section are exercises to assist the students in constructing and creating simple and complex sentences in Tagalog.

Most of the descriptions of the first five chapters are based on *Tagalog Structures* by Teresita Ramos, published by the University Press of Hawaii. All the exercises are new.

Teresita V. Ramos
Resty M. Cena

chapter 1

Tagalog Sounds

Tagalog has 16 consonant sounds, 5 vowel sounds, and 6 diphthongs. Syllable stress is used to distinguish between otherwise similar words. Rising and falling intonation levels at the end of sentences indicate different sentence types.

Consonants

The Tagalog consonants are *b, d, k, g, h, l, m, n, ng, p, ', r, s, t, w,* and *y* . *Ng* represents the velar nasal and the apostrophe ' the glottal stop. The chart below shows the articulatory descriptions of each of the consonants.

Tagalog Consonant Sounds					
	Labial	Dental	Palatal	Velar	Glottal
Stops, Voiceless	*p*	*t*		*k*	'
Stops, Voiced	*b*	*d*		*g*	
Fricatives, Voiceless			*s*		*h*
Nasals, Voiced	*m*	*n*		*ng*	
Laterals, Voiced		*l*			
Flap, Voiced		*r*			
Semi-Vowel, Voiced	*w*		*y*		

Observe the following word pairs:

p / b	*pipi*	dumb	*bibi*	duck
t / d	*kutkot*	scratch	*kudkod*	scrape
k / g	*balak*	plan	*balag*	trellis
k / '	*balik*	return	*bali'*	broken
h /	*hipon*	shrimp	*ipon*	save
s / h	*sipag*	industrious	*hipag*	sister-in-law

1

m / n	sama	go with	sana	hope
n / ng	buno'	wrestle	bungo'	skull
n / l	nasa	desire	lasa	taste
d / r	dilis	fish	rilis	rail
l / r	balat	skin	barat	stingy
w / y	wari'	contemplate	yari'	finished

The Glottal Stop '

The glottal stop ' may cause English speakers some difficulties because it is a sound that does not make a difference in meaning in their language. In Tagalog, however, the glottal stop provides a significant contrast with other sounds. Observe in the examples below its contrast with no sound.

bata	bathrobe	bata'	child
baga	live coal	baga'	lung

The glottal stop is produced when the glottis or the opening between the vocal cords is tightly closed, stopping the air coming from the lungs. It occurs anywhere a consonant may occur except in consonant clusters. If it occurs in word final position, it is marked by the apostrophe in this text.

The glottal stop is generally not indicated in conventional spelling. Words that in written form begin with a vowel when pronounced in isolation actually begin with the glottal stop. Also, what in written form appears to be a sequence of two vowels is actually separated by a glottal stop. Words with a prefix that ends in g and with a stem that begins with the glottal stop, as in mag-inaw 'to soak in' are written with a hyphen. The hyphen forces the pronunciation of the glottal stop. Without the hyphen, the resulting word maginaw 'chilly, cold' means something else.

Exercises

a. Listen to the teacher and identify the words pronounced with a glottal stop.

baga	ember	baga'	lung
bata	robe	bata'	child
tubo	pipe	tubo'	profit
sala	living room	sala'	strain

b. Say the following words aloud.

'umaga	'a'alis	hindi'
'abala	ta'o	tama'
'ikaw	baba'e	wala'
'ako	toto'o	mali'
'umalis	'u'u'wi'	puno'

The Consonant *ng*

The velar nasal *ng* is difficult for an English speaker to produce when it occurs in word or syllable-initial position because it never occurs in this position in English. Examples in initial word and syllable position follow.

ngayon	now	ngiti'	smile
ngipin	tooth	ngiki'	shiver
nganga	open the mouth	nguya'	chew
ngawit	to get tired	ngitngit	irritation

Generally *n* is substituted for *ng* by American learners of Tagalog when the latter occurs in syllable-initial position. The following examples show the two sounds at the beginning of words having different meanings.

ngayon	now	nayon	village
nguya'	chew	nuya'	spite
ngisngis	titter	nisnis	run (say, on stockings)
ngawa'	howl, cry	nawa	may it be so
nga	(a gram. particle)	na	(a gram. particle)
tenga	ear	tena	let's go
sangay	branch	sanay	skilled; used to
pungas	to get up half awake	punas	wipe

Exercises

a. Say the following words aloud.

mga	(pronounced *manga*)	ng	(pronounced *nang*)
langit	heaven	ang	(a grammatical marker)
langitngit	creaking sound	ilong	nose
pangit	ugly	bilang	count

pangalan	name	kulang	lacking
bangos	milkfish	gapang	crawl
tangan	hold	gaspang	coarseness
tango'	nod	'utang	debt

b. In the following words, notice the succession of ng and g, represented in writing as ngg. Pronounce this sequence as you would the sequence ng in the word "bingo."

hanggang	until	langgam	ant
mangga	mango	Inggles	English
Linggo	Sunday	tanggo	tango

c. Try the following phrases and sentences.

magagandang mga ngipin
pangit na pangalan
dalawang magulang
ang mga bilang
Biyernes ngayon; ngumiti ka naman.
Inggo nga ang pangalan niya.
Nagtanggo sina Inggo at Ingga habang nagbibinggo noong isang
   Linggo.
Lumangitngit ang mga ngipin ni Domingga.
Hanggang ngayon lumilingon pa sa pinanggalingan si Ninoy.

The Initial Voiceless Stops *p, t, k*

Tagalog p, t, and k in word-initial position are not aspirated, that is to say, they are pronounced without a puff of air. English p, t, and k in initial word position are aspirated. The English speaker of Tagalog therefore tends to aspirate these sounds. Aspirated p, t, and k do not change the meaning of Tagalog words but if used they give the speaker a foreign accent. Examples of p, t, and k in initial position follow.

p	*t*	*k*
pito	tira	kulay
payat	tubo	kaniya
pangit	tapon	kilay
patak	tubig	kanan
pagpag	totoo	kasi

The *p, t,* and *k* sounds in spark, steam, and scream approximate the pronunciation of the Tagalog *p, t,* and *k*.

Exercises

a. *p/b* Minimal Word Pairs

pata	leg of an animal	bata	robe
patid	break up	batid	know
ipon	save	ibon	bird
lapis	pencil	labis	excess
tapon	throw away	tabon	mound of earth

b. Words with *p/b*

piso	pangalan	batis	balita'
petsa	Pilipinas	baba'	balibag
palengke	pero	biro'	bulag
apat	lapis	taba'	taban
sampo'	kahapon	haba'	laban
sapatos	upa	sabon	ibon
alapaap	kapkap	dibdib	liblib
hirap	harap	talab	loob

c. Phrases and Sentences with *p/b*

apat na piso
bata sa labas
pulang alapaap
labag sa loob
harap-harapanan
ubod nang bilis
Ano ba ang petsa kahapon?
Huwag mong babalibagin ng sabon ang bulag.
Kinapkapan ng pulis nang harap-harapanan ang pari.
May balitang sasabunin ni Billy ang dibdib ng ibon sa batis.

d. Words with *t*

tatay	atin	payat
tama'	natin	sakit

tubig	*bata'*	*malungkot*
tapos	*balita'*	*apat*
tatlo	*matalino*	*pangit*
tukso	*mataba'*	*bakit*
taon	*mataas*	*salamat*
totoo	*mabuti*	*pakiulit*

e.   Phrases and Sentences with *t*

tatlong taon
malungkot na balita'
payat na bata'
matalinong tatay
tatayu-tayo

Tatlong taon nang tatayu-tayu ang tatay sa tabi ng tubo.
Malungkot na balita iyan.
Payat na bata si Tiyago.
Matalino ang Tatay ni Tino.

f.   *k/g* Minimal Word Pairs

kulay	color	*gulay*	vegetable
baka	cow	*baga*	ember
bakal	iron	*bagal*	slow
suko'	surrender	*sugo'*	messenger
tuktok	summit; peak	*tugtog*	play a musical instrment
pakpak	wing	*pagpag*	shake

g.   Words with *k*

kanan	*bakit*	*alak*
kilay	*tiket*	*bulak*
kulay	*wika'*	*anak*
kasi	*bigkas*	*itak*
kutsara	*Pasko*	*patak*
kailan	*akala'*	*itulak*
kaibigan	*katakut-takot*	*ikinagagalak*

h.   Phrases and Sentences with *k*

kanang kamay
kaliwa ng botika

kailan tumahimik
kakaunting-kakaunti'
Kataka-takang mahibang ang katulad mo ay ano?
ikinagagalak kong makilala kayo.
Nakikipagkontest sa kainan ng pakwan si Concordia.
Kiliting-kiliti ang kaluluwa ni Curtis.
Kinikilig at humahagikhik si Kitt.

The Consonant *r*

The *r* in English is retroflexed, that is, the tonque is curled back into the area of the palate. It does not touch the roof of the mouth. The Tagalog *r*, however, is produced with the tongue tapping the gum ridge quickly as happens for the *tt* in Betty for some. Again, as with *p*, *t*, and *k*, pronouncing the English *r* in place of the Tagalog *r* would not change the meaning of the words, but it would affect the clarity of communication. Here are some examples.

renda	*pero*	*lugar*
ronda	*letra*	*asar*
riles	*loro*	*basar*
rito	*mura*	*istar*
rin	*sira'*	*pundar*

The Consonant *l*

The English *l* is produced with the tongue tip at some point along the roof of the mouth, leaving the sides of the tongue open for the air to flow out. The Tagalog *l* on the other hand has the tongue flat from the tip to the back, with the tip back of the upper teeth. Examples of words with *l* follow.

lapit	*alas*	*baol*
lason	*alam*	*burol*
layon	*balik*	*salawal*
langit	*balot*	*kapal*
limot	*lolo*	*legal*
lente	*lola*	*kuntil*
lomo	*kula*	*sugal*
lumot	*kulo'*	*buwal*
lula'	*kaluluwa*	*balabal*
lubi-lubi	*hilung-talilong*	*sagabal*

The Consonants *t, d, n, s*

Tagalog *t, d, n,* and *s* are pronounced with the tongue tip at the back of the upper teeth. English *t, d, n,* and *s* are produced with the tongue tip behind the upper gum ridge. These sounds, pronounced as alveolars rather than as dentals, do not change the meaning of the Tagalog words but may produce some confusion in communication.

Some word pairs showing the contrast between *t* and *d*.

t		*d*	
tuta'	puppy	*duda*	doubt
tagtag	shake	*dagdag*	addition
tastas	unstitched	*dasdas*	pared off
patpat	stick	*padpad*	shipwrecked
pantay	even	*panday*	blacksmith

The rest of the Tagalog consonant sounds *h, b, g, m, y,* and *w* do not cause much difficulty for the speaker of English because they are fairly similar to the corresponding sounds in English.

Vowels

The Tagalog vowel sounds are *i, e, a, o,* and *u.* The vowel chart below shows roughly the tongue height and its fronting or backing in the mouth when each of the vowel sounds is produced.

Tagalog Vowel Sounds			
	Front	Central	Back
High	i		u
Mid	e		o
Low		a	

In phrase-final position, *o* varies freely with *u* and so does *e* with *i.* They are considered separate sounds from *u* and *i* because in a few examples, they distinguish meaning. The mid vowels *e* and *o* are fairly new sounds assimilated in the language from Spanish. Examples of the *u/o* and *i/e* contrasts are as follows.

	e **versus** *i*		
mesa	table	misa	mass
tela	cloth	tila	maybe
benta	sale	binta	moro canoe

	o **versus** *u*		
oso	bear	uso	fad

Exercise

Read the following words and sentences. Pay particular attention to the indicated vowel sound.

a

at	Tagalog	umaga
ang	bahay	asawa
ano	daan	maganda
alam	lahat	pambura

Maala-ala mo kaya, ang sumpa mo sa akin?
Napatihaya si Wanda, dahil bumagsak ang kama.

Ang dalas mag-anak ni Juana; aba, nakakaapat na!
Sinala ni Clara ang salabat sa sala.

e

Ester	mesa	kotse
ewan	petsa	babae
eskuwelahan	papel	lalake
estudyante	Inggles	beynte

i

ito	lapis	si
iyan	bini'	bini-bini'
iyon	sine	gabi
isa	bisita	mabuti

Mabuti at may katabi si Betty.
Malimit bumili ng sili si Igmidio sa palengke.
Ibinaba ni Ester and papel sa mesa kagabi.
Kinindatan ng estudyanteng lalake ang mabining babae.

o

oras	hapon	sino
otso	kotse	impiyerno
opo'	tuloy	kayo
onse	hoy	libro

u	ulo	head	ulu	head
	u'od	worm	u'ud	worm
	bu'o'	whole	bu'u'	whole
	bakod	fence	bakud	fence

Ubod nang baho' ang u'od.

Lumuhod si Alponso sa bakod mula alas-otso hanggang alas-onse.

Magbukod ka ng buko para kay Julio.

Uupu-upo, tatayu-tayo, lalaru-laro, kaya, hayan, sumakit tuloy ang ulo.

Diphthongs

The Tagalog diphthongs are *iw, ey, ay, aw, oy,* and *uy.* Diphthongs are complex sounds which are combinations of simple vowel sounds and semi-vowels.

Tagalog Diphthongs

	Front	Central	Back
High	iw		uy
Mid	ey		oy
Low		ay aw	

Except for *iw* and *uy* all the Tagalog diphthongs have their corresponding sounds in English. The diphthong *iw* in word-final position may cause problems in production because speakers of English tend to break the diphthong into two syllables. Thus *sisiw* 'chick' may become the incorrect *sisiyew.* In word-medial position, the diphthong is broken into the component sounds, and the semi-vowel serves as the initial sound of the following syllable.

Exercise

Say the following words aloud.

baliw	crazy	aruy	Ouch!
giliw	darling	kasuy	cashew

bitiw	let go	*tsapsuy*	chop suey
aliw	amuse	*tsampuy*	preserved fruit

Malaking kabaliwan!
Aba, bumitiw ka naman sa iyong giliw.
Nilagyan ni Ninoy ng kasuy ang tsapsuy.
Nakagat ni Pinay ang siling labuyo, aruy!
Araw-araw, ngumunguyngoy si Nonoy kung wala siyang
tsampuy.

Stress and Vowel Length

Stress in Tagalog roots is usually on either of the last two syllables. But it needs an exhaustive study to find out on which of these two syllables it falls in any particular root. Stressed syllables, except for final ones, are accompanied by vowel length. In the examples below, the colon : after a vowel indicates lengthening. Note the absence of vowel lengthening in the final syllable in the last two examples.

báhay	*ba:hay*	house
asáwa	*asa:wa*	spouse
pulá	*pula*	pula
salitá'	*salita'*	word; speak

The following pairs of words show that a shift in stress results in a difference in meaning.

Stress on First Syllable		**Stress on Second Syllable**	
áso	dog	*asó*	smoke
bálat	birthmark	*balát*	skin
búkas	tomorrow	*bukás*	open
káyo	cloth	*kayó*	you (pl.)
gábi	yam	*gabí*	night
hámon	a dare	*hamón*	ham
páko'	nail	*pakó'*	fern
páso'	a burn	*pasó'*	flower pot
sáya	skirt	*sayá*	gaiety
túbo	pipe	*tubó*	sugar cane

Exercise

Indicate the correct stress of the words in boldface.

1. *Natakot ang **aso** sa **aso**.*   dog / smoke
2. *May **balat** siya sa **balat**.*   birthmark / skin
3. ***Bukas** ang **bukas** ng tindahan.*   tomorrow / open
4. ***Gabi** ang kain niya ng **gabi**.*   night / yam
5. *Nakasabit sa **pako** ang **pako**.*   nail / fern
6. *Dalhin mo ang **laruan** sa **laruan**.*   toy / playground
7. *Ang **saya** niya nang matapos ang **saya**.* happy / skirt
8. *Pinukpok niya ng **tubo** ang **tubo**.*   pipe / sugar cane
9. *Galing sa mainit na **paso** ang **paso** niya.* flower pot / burn
10. ***Hapon** dumadalaw ang **Hapón**.*   afternoon / Japanese

Some Tagalog Sound Changes

Deletion of Non-Final Glottal Stop

In rapid speech, the glottal stop within words and the final glottal stop within phrases or sentences may disappear.

> sa'an   Saan ka ba nagpunta?
> basa'   Basa siya kanina.

Exercise

Say the words and phrases aloud. Pay attention to the loss of non-final ' in the phrases.

baba'	ang baba-baba'	very low
bata'	ang bata-bata'	very young
haba'	ang haba-haba'	very long
dali'	ang dali-dali'	very easy
ikli'	ang ikli-ikli'	very short
puti'	ang puti-puti'	very white
tanda'	ang tanda-tanda'	very old
'ito	Ano ito?	
'iyan	Ano iyan?	

'iyon	Ano iyon?
'umaga	Magandang umaga.
tanghali'	Magandang tanghali po'.
bintana'	Bintana po ito.
po'	Si Belen po siya.
wala'	Wala pong anuman.

Raising of Vowel Sounds

The vowel *e* raises to *i* and the vowel *o* to *u* in non-final position. (One may also view this as a process of lowering.)

babae	babaing maganda
lalake	lalaking matapang
ale	Aling Nena
tale'	taling mahigpit
pare'	paring mabait
balot	balutin
halo'	haluin
biro'	biruin
bilog	bilugin
talop	talupan

In reduplicated words, the *u/o* alternation is strongly observed but less so with the front vowels *i/e*.

biro'	biru-biro'
halo'	halu-halo'
sari'	sari-sari'
unti'	unti-unti'

Alternation of *d* and *r*

The consonant *d* often becomes *r* between vowels in affixation or even across word boundaries in phrase and sentence formation.

kudku**d**	kudku**r**an
dating	da**r**ating
daan	apat na **r**aan

Exercises

a. *Daan* means a unit of hundred. Its variant form when preceded by a vowel is *raan.* Supply the missing *d* / *r* in the following.

isang	?aan	(100)
dalawang	?aan	(200)
tatlong	?aan	(300)
apat na	?aan	(400)
limang	?aan	(500)
anim na	?aan	(600)
pitong	?aan	(700)
walong	?aan	(800)
siyam na	?aan	(900)

b. Combine the following roots and affixes.

1. *ka + da + dating*

2. *na + doon*

3. *na + dito*

4. *ka + dugtong*

5. *ka + dunong + an*

Sound Changes in Affixation

The *Mang-* Prefix

The final nasal sound of the affix *mang-* undergoes some changes as it gets influenced by the following initial sound of the root. This change may also be followed by the loss of the first consonant of the root. Observe the following changes:

       mang + pili' =>   *mampili'*   (make *ng* "similar" to *p*, giving *m*)
                    =>   *mamili'*   (now drop the root's initial consonant *p*)

Similarly:

       mang + bili   =>   *mamili*
       mang + takot =>   *manakot*

mang + dalangin => manalangin
mang + kuha' => manguha'
mang +'isda' => mangisda'

The sounds h and g do not influence the final nasal of the prefix mang.

mang + gulo => manggulo
mang + huli => manghuli

Exercise

Make the changes in the following combinations.

1. mang + tukso — to tease
2. mang + suntok — to hit with the fist
3. mang + bundok — to seek refuge in the mountains
4. mang + 'utang — to borrow money
5. mang + palengke — to do the grocery shopping
6. mang + gapang — to crawl
7. mang + hiram — to borrow
8. mang + kailangan — to be in need
9. mang + pulot — to pick up
10. mang + budbud — to sprinkle, to distribute
11. mang + bigay — to give
12. mang + 'itlog — to lay eggs
13. mang + 'aso — to hunt
14. mang + damit — to dress up
15. mang +dikit — to stick together

Verb bases with initial consonant l and a few bases with d retain these sounds after the final nasal of mang has undergone the sound change.

mang + likum => manlikum to gather
mang + damo => mandamo to pull the weeds
mang + dukot => mandukot to pick pockets

mang + *linlang*	=>	*manlinlang*	to deceive
mang + *lito*	=>	*manlito*	to confuse
mang + *loko*	=>	*manloko*	to deceive
mang + *dagok*	=>	*mandagok*	to hit with the fist

The stressed affix *mang-*, prefixed to the root plus a reduplication of the second syllable of the stem (after the assimilation and loss of the initial consonant of the root have taken place), indicates occupation or a habitual kind of work.

prefix + root	assimilation	redup of the 2nd syl	
mang + *sayaw* =>	*manayaw*	=> *mananayaw*	dancer
mang + *kulot* =>	*mangulot*	=> *mangungulot*	hairdresser

When the initial consonant of the base is not lost like *g* and *h*, and occasionally *k*, the first consonant - vowel sequence of the root is reduplicated.

mang + *hula'*	=>	*manghuhula'*	fortune-teller
mang + *gawa'*	=>	*manggagawa'*	maker
mang + *kulam*	=>	*mangkukulam*	sorcerer

Exercise

Construct terms for occupation or habitual kind of work from the following.

1.	*mang* + *singil*	bill collector
2.	*mang* + *dukot*	pickpocket
3.	*mang* + *gamot*	doctor
4.	*mang* + *'isda'*	fisherman
5.	*mang* + *tahi'*	seamstress
6.	*mang* + *bili*	buyer
7.	*mang* + *kanta*	singer
8.	*mang* + *digma*	warrior
9.	*mang* + *dugo*	bogey man
10.	*mang* + *baril*	hunter

The *Pang-* Prefix

Pang- undergoes the same changes for the final nasal as does *mang-*:

- When *pang-* is affixed to root words starting with *p, b,* or *m,* the final *ng* of *pang-* becomes *m,* for example, *pang + butas => pambutas.*
- When attached to roots starting with *t, d,* or *n,* the final ng becomes *n,* for example, *pang + damo => pandamo.*
- When prefixed to root words starting with *g, ng,* or *h,* and vowel sounds (actually the glottal stop), the *ng* of *pang-* remains unchanged, for example, *pang + hiwa' => panghiwa'.*

Exercise

Following the example, give the *pang- ...-in* forms of the following roots.

Example: *pang + pili'+ in => pamiliin* to have someone choose

1. *pang + tahi' + in*   to have someone sew
2. *pang + 'itlog + in*   to make (a hen) lay eggs
3. *pang + 'isda' in*   to have someone go fishing
4. *pang + 'anak + in*   to help someone give birth
5. *pang + kislap + in*   to make something shine

Pang- expresses the instrument used for performing what the root word denotes.

butas	hole	*pambutas*	instrument used for boring holes
hiwa'	cut	*panghiwa'*	instrument used for cutting
punas	wipe	*pamunas*	instrument used for wiping

Exercise

Supply the missing instruments.

1.	*linis*	clean	*panglinis*	instrument for cleaning
2.	*palo'*	spank		instrument for spanking
3.	*takot*	fear		instrument for scaring someone

4.	*pukpok*	pound	instrument for pounding
5.	*giling*	ground	instrument for grinding
6.	*huli*	catch	instrument for catching
7.	*kuha*	get	instrument for getting
8.	*damo*	grass	instrument for weeding
9.	*sulat*	write	instrument for writing
10.	*sukat*	measure	instrument for measuring

Pang- may be used to form ordinals.

pang + dalawa	=>	*pangalawa*	second
pang + tatlo	=>	*pangatlo*	third
pang + 'apat	=>	*pang-'apat*	fourth
pang + lima	=>	*panlima*	fifth
pang + 'anim	=>	*pang-'anim*	sixth
pang + pito	=>	*pampito*	seventh
pang + walo	=>	*pangwalo*	eight
pang + siyam	=>	*pansiyam*	ninth
pang + sampo'	=>	*pansampo'*	tenth

The *Ipang-* Affix

The final nasal sound of the *ipang-* affix undergoes the same changes undergone by the *ipang-* affix: *ipang + butas => ipambutas* 'to use for boring holes.'

Exercise

Supply the *ipang-* form of the following roots.

1.	*punas*	to wipe	*ipangpunas*	to use for wiping
2.	*suklay*	to comb		to use for combing
3.	*linis*	to clean		to use for cleaning
4.	*sandok*	to ladle		to use for scooping food
5.	*hiwa'*	to cut		to use for cutting

5.	*dikdik*	to pound	to use for pounding
6.	*hawak*	to hold	to use for holding
7.	*gawa'*	to make	to use for making
8.	*halo'*	to stir	to use for stirring

-Ng after *Labi*

Labi, derived from *labis* 'more or over,' is added to the cardinals from *isa* 'one' to *siyam* 'nine' to mean 'eleven' to 'nineteen.' Depending upon the following sound, the *-ng* may have the *-n* or *-m* alternate forms.

> *-ng* before vowel sounds and *w*
> *-n* before *d, t, l* or *s*
> *-m* before *p*

Exercise

Supply the correct form of the linker.

1.	*labi + ng + isa*	=>	eleven
2.	*labi + ng + dalawa*	=>	twelve
3.	*labi + ng + tatlo*	=>	thirteen
4.	*labi + ng + 'apat*	=>	fourteen
5.	*labi + ng + lima*	=>	fifteen
6.	*labi + ng + 'anim*	=>	sixteen
7.	*labi + ng + pito*	=>	seventeen
8.	*labi + ng + walo*	=>	eighteen
9.	*labi + ng + siyam*	=>	nineteen

The Sound *h* in the Suffixes *-in* and *-an*

When the verb base ends in a vowel sound, the suffixes *-an* and *-in* become *-han* and *-hin*, respectively.

> *kanta + an* => *kantahan*
> *kanta + in* => *kantahin*

Exercise

a. Supply -an or -han to the following roots.

1. *dala*   to carry
2. *bili*   to buy
3. *lagay*   to place
4. *punas*   to wipe
5. *kuha*   to get (note: the resulting form is irregular)

b. Supply -in or -hin to the following roots.

1. *huli*   to catch
2. *abot*   to reach
3. *sabi*   to say
4. *sukat*   to measure
5. *kuha*   to get (note: the resulting form is irregular)

Stress Shift Due to Suffixation

In suffixation, stress shifts to the next syllable.

> *básа + in basáhin*   to read
> *sagót + in sagutín*   to answer

A rare exception: *kópya + in => kópyahin* 'to copy.'

Exercise

Indicate the stress in the suffixed forms below.

1. *búhat*   buhatin
2. *gupit*   gupitin
3. *burá*   burahin

4. *sípa'*	*sipain*
5. *lúto'*	*lutuin*
6. *hingí'*	*hingiin*
7. *áyos*	*ayusin*
8. *kálong*	*kalungin*
9. *lápad*	*laparan*
10. *sagót*	*sagutin*

Syllable Reduction Due to Suffixation

Some word bases drop their final unstressed vowels when the *-in* / *-an* form is suffixed to the root. The reduced form is more common in speech.

labá + an	*labahán*	*labhan*	to wash
bilí + in	*bilihín*	*bilhin*	to buy
dalá + in	*dalahín*	*dalhin*	to bring
gawá' + in	*gawa'ín*	*gawin*	to make
hingí' + in	*hingi'ín*	*hingin*	to ask for

Note the loss of the glottal stop, as in the last two examples. Also, note the exceptional change in *kuha*, which becomes *kunin* and *kunan.*

Alternation between *-in-* and *ni-*

In verb bases that begin with *l-*, the infix *-in-*, indicating completed action, changes to *ni-* and is prefixed to the base to form the completed and incompleted aspects. For some bases this is an optional change, for others mandatory. When in doubt perform the change.

lininis	*nilinis*	cleaned
linaro	*nilaro*	played with
linuto'	*niluto'*	cooked
linimot	*nilimot*	forgot
linoko	*niloko*	fooled

Pitch and Intonation

Tagalog sentences vary slightly in pitch. A sentence usually starts off with a **normal** pitch, going up slightly over stressed syllables, reaching a **high** pitch when the sentence is a question, or ending in a normal or even **low** pitch if a statement.

Tagalog sentences vary even less with respect to intonation. Intonation **rises** for questions and requests, **falls** or levels off for statements, commands, and responses, and **suspends** for series and non-final phrases.

In general, when in doubt, use the normal pitch and the normal level in any sentence types. Your speech may sound monotonous, but hopefully not foreign.

Exercise

Imitate your teacher as he or she reads the following sentences. Draw lines across the sentences to indicate pitch and intonation.

Statements

> *Malamig ang tubig.*
>
> *Malakas ang ulan.*
>
> *Naupo ang turista.*
>
> *Sumakay si Ben sa diyep.*

Yes-No Questions

> *Malamig ba ang tubig?*
>
> *Malakas ba ang ulan?*
>
> *Naupo ba ang turista?*
>
> *Sumakay ba si Ben sa diyep?*
>
> *Aalis ka, di ba?*
>
> *Magulo si Abraham, di ba?*

Information Questions

    Alin ang anak mo?

    Saan ka nakatira?

    Sino si Honasan?

Requests

    Pakiabot nga ng asin?

    Pakisara nga ng pinto?

    Pakidala nga ng libro ko?

Commands

    Hinto!

    Kunin mo ang pangalan niya.

    Huwag mong balibagin ang mangga.

Phrases in Sequence

    Isa, dalawa, tatlo, ang Tatang mong kalbo.

    Pumunta ka sa palengke at bumili ka ng suka, kamatis, at bagoong.

Responses

    Oo, (Amerikano nga si Jorge).

    Hindi, (hindi siya tamad).

    Si Dante.

chapter 2

Simple Sentences

Three general classes of simple sentences will be discussed: sentences with a subject, subjectless sentences, and existential sentences. Subjectless sentences and existentials have fewer structure types than sentences with a subject, but they, too, occur extensively in common speech. The learner is well-advised to become familiar with all three sentence types.

Sentences with a Subject

The typical simple sentence in Tagalog has a subject (or topic) and a predicate (or comment about the topic). The normal order of these elements is Predicate then Subject. In contrast, in English the order is Subject then Predicate.

Predicate	Subject	
Tumakbo	*si John.*	John ran.
Maganda	*si Sue.*	Sue is pretty.
Doktor	*ang bisita.*	The guest is a doctor.
Nasa kusina	*ang relo.*	The clock is in the kitchen.

The Subject

The subject can be a noun, a pronoun, a demonstrative, an adjective, a verb, or a prepositional phrase.

Noun Subject   In terms of the way they are marked, noun subjects divide into two general classes: personal names marked by *si* versus all other nouns, which are marked by *ang*. Examples of sentences with personal nouns as subjects:

	Marker	Personal Noun
Ngumiti	*si*	*Perla.*
Lumaban	*si*	*Daniel.*
Lumundag	*si*	*Tagpi.*
Ngumiyaw	*si*	*Muning.*

The last two examples have subjects which are personalized names of a dog and a cat. Non-human animate subjects when personalized are marked by *si.*

Non-personal nouns are marked by *ang.* These are common nouns and any inanimate nouns including what, in English, are considered as proper nouns, such as names of places, buildings, books, etc.

	Marker	Non-Personal Nouns
Ngumiti	*ang*	*dalaga.*
Lumaban	*ang*	*sundalo.*
Lumundag	*ang*	*aso.*
Ngumiyaw	*ang*	*pusa.*
Umuunlad	*ang*	*Maynila.*
Palabas	*ang*	Star Trek.
Malungkot	*ang*	Noli Me Tangere.

Kin terms and civic terms are marked by either *ang* or *si. Ang* is less personal and a bit more respectful.

	Marker	Kin Terms
Dumating	*si / ang*	*Tatay.*
Nagagalit	*si / ang*	*Nanay.*
Nagtatampo	*si / ang*	*Ate.*
Naglaro	*si / ang*	*Kuya.*

	Marker	Civic Terms
Darating	*si / ang*	*Presidente.*
Nagsalita	*si / ang*	*Gobernador.*
Kakandidato uli	*si / ang*	*Mayor.*

The plural of personal nouns is formed by replacing the marker *si* with *sina.* The plural of non-personal nouns is formed by adding *mga* (pronounced *ma-nga*) to *ang.*

	Noun Markers	
	Singular	**Plural**
Personal	si	sina
Non-personal	ang	ang mga

Kumain	**ang mga**	bisita.
Bumalik	**ang mga**	sulat.
Namasyal	**sina**	Donna. (Donna and others)

Non-personal proper nouns may also be pluralized, although the need for it seldom arises.

> Magkakasinglaki **ang mga** San Fernando.
> The San Fernando (towns) are of the same size.

Common nouns may be personified. They take the personal marker si.

		Personified
	Marker	**Common Nouns**
Pumasok na	**si**	Estudyante.
Dumalaw pala	**si**	Sundalo.

Personal names can be used as common nouns, in which case the marker ang is used, as well as the form mga when plural.

Maganda **ang** Marilyn.	The (name) Marilyn is pretty.
Magaganda lahat **ang mga** Marilyn.	All the Marilyns are pretty.
Masisipag **ang mga** Juan dito.	The Juans here are industrious.

Exercise

Supply the missing marker ang or si. The plural form of ang is ang mga and si is sina.

1. Nagluto   ang   babae.

2. Matapang   sundalo. (plural)

3. Uminom   bata.

4. Inhinyero   Damian.

5.	*Nasa bahay*	*Nanay.*
6.	*Masipag*	*Marsha at Nina.*
7.	*Naiwan*	*estudyante.* (plural)
8.	*Umalis*	*katulong.*
9.	*Nabasag*	*banga.*
10.	*Sa Linggo*	*kasal.*

Pronoun Subject   The forms of pronoun subjects are distinguished according to person: **first**, **second**, or **third**, and number: **singular** or **plural**. In the first person plural, an added distinction is made between **exclusive** (excluding the hearer) and **inclusive** (including the hearer). Pronouns are not preceded by *ang* or *si*.

Pronoun Subject Set		
	Singular	**Plural**
1st Person	*ako*	*kami* (exclusive)
		tayo (inclusive)
2nd Person	*ikaw/ka*	*kayo*
3rd Person	*siya*	*sila*

Matipid **siya.**
Magpipiknik **kami.**
Lumakad na **tayo.**
Nasiyahan **ako.**

Ikaw usually occurs initially while *ka* occurs elsewhere.

Bumila **ka** *ng saging.*
Ikaw *ba ang bagong dating?*

The form *kita* (*kata* in some dialects), not in the chart above, refers to the singular hearer and the speaker. It is also used in place of the subject and the object in sentences like "I saw you."

Kita *nga e mag-usap.*	Let's the two of us talk.
Mag-usap nga **kita.**	Let's the two of us talk.

*Nakita **kita** = Nakita **ko ikaw**.*	I saw you.
*Ipagdadasal **kita**.*	I'll say a prayer for you.

Exercises

a. Complete the following sentences by adding subjects appropriate for the marker.

1. *Batang-bata   ang sundalo.*
2. *Batang-bata   si*
3. *Nasa labas   si*
4. *Nasa labas   ang*
5. *Natulog   ang*
6. *Natulog   si*
7. *Nars   si*
8. *Nars   ang*
9. *Tumawa   ang*
10. *Tumawa   si*

b. Instead of nouns, use pronouns as indicated by their English equivalents below to complete the sentences in the previous exercise.

1. they   *Batang-bata sila.*
2. we (exclusive)
3. she
4. he
5. you (singular)
6. you (plural)
7. I
8. we (inclusive)
9. he and she
10. you (singular) and I

Demonstrative Subject   Demonstratives indicate the relative distance of objects from the speaker and the listener.

Demonstrative Subject Set
ito	this
iyan	that
iyon	that yonder

In rapid speech, the *i-* of the demonstrative is dropped. The plural forms are constructed by adding *ang mga* before the demonstratives.

Singular Demonstrative Subject		Plural Demonstrative Subject	
Itapon mo	**ito.**	*Itapon mo*	**ang mga** *ito.*
Basahin mo	**iyan.**	*Basahan mo*	**ang mga** *iyan.*
Kunin mo	**iyon.**	*Kunin mo*	**ang mga** *iyon.*

Exercise

Change the subject into its pronoun or demonstrative substitute.

1.	*Nagluto*	siya.	(babae)
2.	*Mapag-isip*		(*sundalo* plural)
3.	*Umiinom*		(*bata*)
4.	*Inhinyero*		(Roberta)
5.	*Nasa bahay*		(*nanay*)
6.	*Adbenturera*		(Marta *at* Nina)
7.	*Pumasa*		(*estudyante* plural)
8.	*Nagpa-alam*		(*bisita*)
9.	*Nabasag*		(*banga'* plural)
10.	*Sa Linggo*		(*ang lakad*)

Adjective Subject The form of the basic Tagalog adjective is *ma* + root.

Adjective Prefix		Root	
ma	+	hirap	mahirap
ma	+	dali	madali
ma	+	lupit	malupit

When used as subject, adjectives are preceded by the subject marker *ang*.

	Singular Adjective Subject
Kawawa	ang mahirap.
Magbabayad	ang malupit.

When in the plural, the first consonant and vowel of the root is reduplicated; *mga* is optionally added after the marker *ang*.

	Plural Adjective Subject
Kawawa	ang **mga** mahihirap.
Magbabayad	ang **mga** malulupit.

Roots that can be used as adjectives without adjectival prefix can only be pluralized by the addition of *mga* to the marker. It is incorrect to reduplicate the first consonant-vowel of the root.

Correct:	Incorrect:
Na-gong ang mga pangit.	Na-gong ang mga *papangit.
Nauntog ang mga pandak.	Nauntog ang mga *papandak.

Verbal Subject Verbs can also be used as subject. They are preceded by the subject marker *ang*, and additionally by *mga* when plural.

	Singular Verb Subject		Plural Verb Subject
Naubusan	ang natulog.	Naubusan	ang mga natulog.
Naghanda na	ang lalangoy.	Naghanda na	ang mga lalangoy.
Nasaktan	ang nadulas.	Nasaktan	ang mga nadulas.
Umani	ang nagtanim.	Umani	ang mga nagtanim.

The verbal subject phrase is equivalent to the English construction "the one who ate," "the one who slept," etc. Thus the whole sentence can be given a complex sentence analysis.

Exercises

a. Change the following into sentences having adjective or verbal subjects.

1. *Nakita rin ang batang nawawala.*
   Nakita rin ang nawawala.
2. *Binayaran ang taong nagkumpune.*

3. *Nahuli ang taong nagnakaw.*

4. *Dinala sa ospital ang taong nasagasaan.*

5. *Napili ang estudyanteng marunong.*

6. *Nalason ang taong kumain.*

7. *Nasamid ang trabahador na nag-aapura.*

8. *Nahulog ang manlalarong magulo.*

9. *Inape ang taong mahirap.*

10. *Masuwerte ang taong mabait.*

b. Change all singular adjective subjects into plural in the preceding exercise.

Prepositional Phrases as Subject   Prepositional phrases can also be used as subject.

Nahulog	*ang **nasa kusina.***
Nabasag	*ang **kay John.***
Nalusaw	*ang **para kay Madonna.***
*Na-*approve	*ang **tungkol sa** strike.*

These phrases can be given both singular and plural readings. When the subject phrase expresses location, its plurality can be made explicit by the addition of *mga* to the marker.

Explicit Plural
(only when phrase is locative)

Nahulog	*ang* **mga** *nasa kusina.*
Nabasag	*ang* **mga** *nasa kahon.*
*Nag-*worry	*ang* **mga** *nasa Maynila.*

The Predicate

The Predicate can be a verb, an adjective, a noun, or a prepositional phrase.

Verbal Predicate

Nahulog	*si Bill.*
Tinamaan	*ang ibon.*
Lalangoy	*sila.*

Adjectival Predicate

Batugan	*si Bill.*
Malabsa'	*ang kanin.*
Bulok	*ang repolyo.*

Nominal Predicate

Boksingero	*si Mike.*
Nars	*ang* girlfriend *niya.*

Prepositional Predicate

Nasa kusina	*si Rafael.*
Para sa Nanay	*ang regalo.*
Sa Sabado	*ang parada.*
Bukas	*ang laro.*
Mamaya	*iyon.*

Time expressions like *bukas, mamaya, kahapon,* etc. are treated as prepositional phrases, although they do not show a preposition-like marker.

Exercise

a. Complete the following sentences by supplying the missing predicates.

1. Verbal

Ngumiti *ang titser.*

si Ben.

kayo.

2. Nominal

        ang babae.

        siya.

        sina Rita.

3. Adjectival

        ang libro.

        si Marie.

        ang balita.

4. Prepositional

        ang relo.

        iyon.

        ang mga masusuwerte.

Subjectless Sentences

The *ang* phrase, which serves as the subject of the sentence, does not occur in a special set of sentences. In these sentences, none of the participants in the event is subject or focus of the sentence.

Gusto Sentences

Sentences with *gusto* 'like, want,' followed by a noun phrase functioning as object or goal, do not require a subject when the object is indefinite.

	Non-Subject Actor	Non-Subject Indefinite Object
Gusto	*ng bisita*	*ng litson.*
Gusto	*ni Dan*	*ng halu-halo.*
Gusto	*ni Mrs. Santos*	*ng Winter.*

When the object is definite, it must be the subject.

	Actor	Subject Definite Object
Gusto	*ng bisita*	**ang** *litson.*
Gusto	*ni Dan*	**ang** *halu-halo.*
Gusto	*ni Mrs. Santos*	**ang** *Winter.*

When a verb is present in the *gusto* sentence in a construction similar to the English "likes to eat," or "likes to hike," the actor-focus verb requires no subject, whereas the object-focus verb requires a subject. Notice the linker *na/-ng* after the actor.

> *Gusto ni Dan* **na** *kumain ng litson.*
> *Gusto ni Pedro***ng** *kainin ang litson.*

Ibig and *nais* are synonyms of *gusto.* Avoid the stilted *nais.* The negative of *gusto* is *ayaw.*

> **Ayaw** *ng tsuper ng ulan.*
> **Ibig** *mo ba ng tubig?*

Exercises

a. Write *gusto* or *ayaw* sentences about the following object and actor phrases.

1. *gulay* / he   ***Gusto niya ng gulay.***

2. *gatas* / I

3. *adobo* / we (excl.)

4. *kanin* / we (incl.)

5. *isda* / Carlos

6. *pinya* / bisita

7. *alak* / they

8. *balut* / you (pl.)

9. *bagoong* / you (sg.)

10. *ampalaya* / this one

b. Add subjects where necessary.

1. *Gusto niyang inumin...*

2. *Gusto kong lumangoy...*

3. *Ayaw ni Rosang kantahin...*

4. *Gusto ng kaibigan kong tumakbo...*

5. *Gusto ng anak niyang bumili ng bagong kotse...*

6. *Gusto ng batang maglaro...*

7. *Gusto ng estudyanteng basahin...*

8. *Ayaw niyang isauli sa akin...*

9. *Gusto niyang iluto...*

10. *Ayaw niyang maglaba...*

Phenomenal Sentences

Sentences whose predicates consist of verbs stating certain acts of nature, when inflected as *-um-* verbs, don't show a subject phrase.

Umulan.	It rained.
Umulan nang malakas.	It rained hard.
Umuulan sa bundok.	It is raining in the mountains.

Other roots in this class are:

araw	sun	*Umaaraw na!*
ambon	drizzle	*Umambon kanina.*
kulog	thunder	*Kumulog kamakalawa.*
kidlat	lightning	*Kumidlat na naman.*
lindol	earthquake	*Lumilindol yata.*
baha	flood	*Bumaha sa Maynila.*
hangin	wind	*Humangin sa bukid.*
bagyo	typhoon	*Bumagyo sa Cebu.*
dilim	darkness	*Dumilim sa salas.*
liwanag	light	*Lumiwanag sa kusina.*

The last two roots allow some flexibility in that they may also show a subject phrase.

*Dumilim **ang** panahon.*
*Lumiwanag **ang** panahon.*

Indeed, they seem to belong to a class by themselves in that they are the only two roots in this class that accept the verbal affix *nag-*.

Nagdilim sa salas.　　　　　　*Nagdilim ang salas.*
Nagliwanag sa kusina.　　　　*Nagliwanag ang kusina.*

Phenomenal roots, when inflected as *-in-* verbs, require a subject phrase.

	Subject
Binaha	*ang Maynila.*
Nilindol *	*ang San Francisco.*
Binagyo	*ang Tahiti.*

*Remember, *-in-* becomes *ni-* in roots beginning with the sound *l.*

Of course when these words are used in the non-phenomenal sense, they require a subject phrase even when taking the *-um-* affix.

	Subject
Lumiwanag	*ang mukha ni Joaquin.*
Dumilim	*ang pag-asa ni Grant.*
Bumaha	*ang alak sa kasalan.*
Kumulog	*ang boses ni Daniel.*
Humangin	*na naman si Ben.*

Sentences that refer to time or phases of the day are also subjectless.

Tanghali na.
Katanghalian na.
Alas-tres na pala.
Alas-singko na ngayon sa L.A.
Gabi na naman.
Hatinggabi na pala.
Madaling-araw na.
Umaga na.

Similarly, when inflected as *-in-* verbs, they require a subject.

Ginabi si Mario.
Inumaga si Damian sa madyungan.
Hinapon si Ramon sa trabaho.
Hinatinggabi si Ursula.
Inalas-singko ang guwardia.

Exercise

a. Translate the following into Tagalog using phenomenal verbs.

Example: There is an earthquake (*lindol*) going on.
        Lumilindol.

1. The sun (*araw*) will shine tomorrow.

2. There was a storm (*bagyo*) last Sunday.

3. There will be a flood (*baha*) soon.

4. It's drizzling (*ambon*).

5. Strong winds (*hangin*) are blowing in the Galapagos.

b. Complete the following sentences with the correct form of the time words.

Example: *Madalas siyang **inuumaga**. (umaga)* .

1.   (*tanghali*) *na naman siya.*

2. *Tuwing Biyernes*   (*gabi*) *siya.*

3.   (*umaga*) *na naman siya sa trabaho.*

4. *Ewan kung bakit siya laging*   (*gabi*) *nang dating.*

5.   (*hapon*) *nang uwi si Andres.*

Sentences with *ka-* Verbs

Ka- marks a recently completed action of the verb. Like the rest of the sentences in this section, it has no subject phrase. It is often followed by the adverbial particle *lang*. The recently completed aspect is formed by the affix *ka-* followed by the reduplicated first consonant-vowel of the verb root. The reduplication signals action started.

> *ka + li + linis*
> *ka + a + alis*
> *Ka + ba + balik lang ni Lourdes.*   Lourdes just returned.
> *Ka + si + simba lang ni Marco.*   Marco just heard mass.

Exercises

a. Change the following into recently completed verb forms.

Example: *pasyal   kapapasyal*

1. *upo*
2. *basa*
3. *inom*
4. *prito*
5. *plano*

b. Translate the following.

Example:
  I have just eaten (*kain*) breakfast.
  Kakakain ko lang ng almusal.

1. Father just arrived (*dating*) recently.

2. He has just cleaned (*linis*) the house.

3. They have just taken their exams (*iksamen*).

4. Mrs. Santos has just opened (*bukas*) her store.

5. I have just been (*punta*) to Maynila.

Exclamation Sentences

Sentences in which the predicate or its adverbial modifier is made the focus of an exclamation have no subject. The focus word is marked by *ang*.

Ang bilis ng babae!	How fast the woman is!
Ang takbo ni Ben!	How Ben ran!
Ang bilis tumakbo ni Ben.	How fast Ben ran (runs)!

To turn a simple sentence into an exclamation sentence:

- Replace the subject marker with a non-subject marker
  *Mahusay **ang** mekaniko.*   *... **ng** mekaniko.*
- Remove the affixes of the adjective or verb modifier
  ***Ma**husay ang mekaniko*   *... husay ng mekaniko.*
- Introduce the sentence with an exclamation marker.
  Mahusay ang mekaniko   ***Ang** husay ng mekaniko.*

Adjectives are the most common word bases in this construction. Adverb and verb word bases also occur.

Adverb Base

Mabilis tumakbo si Bjorn.	*Ang bilis tumakbo ni Bjorn.*
Mabagal lumakad si Josefa.	*Ang bagal lumakad ni Josefa.*
Malapad ngumiti si Martina.	*Anong lapad ngumiti ni Martina.*

Verb Base

Tumakbo si Kurt.	*Ang takbo ni Kurt!*
Umiyak si Martin.	*Ang iyak ni Martin!*
Tumawa ang babae.	*Ang tawa ng babae.*

When the focused word is an adjective or an adverb, the marker *anong* and *kay* may be used instead of *ang*.

> **Anong** bilis ni Ben.
> **Kay** yaman ng Sultan.

These markers may not combine with focused verbs.

> ***Anong** takbo ni Ben.
> ***Kay** kain ni Dante.

When a verb has an adverbial modifier, only the modifier can serve as the focus of the exclamation sentence.

Mabilis umusad si Nina.	*Ang bilis umusad ni Nina.*
	**Ang mabilis usad ni Nina.*

To express the strongest exclamation, reduplicate the adjective root, prefix it with *pagka-*, and introduce the sentence with *anong*.

> *Anong pagkabilis-bilis ni Ben!*
> *Anong pagkayaman-yaman ng sultan!*
> *Anong pagkasama-sama naman ng kaibigan ko!*

Exercises

a. Change the following sentences into exclamation sentences introduced by *kay, ang,* or *anong.*

1. *Suwabe si Dale.*   ***Anong suwabe ni Dale.***

2. *Magastos ang boss ko.*

3. *Mahal ang kotse ni Mayor.*

4. *Mahusay makisama si Brent.*

5. *Mabagal ang asenso ko.*

6. *Masuwerte si Oswaldo.*

7. *Lumundag siya.*

8. *Matalas ang dila ni Eldo.*

9. *Umiyak ang tindera.*

10. *Nagalit ang hepe.*

11. *Tumawa si Jonathan.*

12. *Tumakbo ako.*

13. *Mabilis mag-isip si Tarcila.*

14. *Madaling pakiusapan si Roberto.*

15. *Naawa ako kay Nonoy.*

b. Express the first five exclamations using *Anong pagka-.*

1.

2.

3.

4.

5.

Intensive Sentences

An adjective predicate or an adverbial modifer may be intensified by dropping their affixes and prefixing *napaka-* to the root. The subject marker is replaced by the appropriate non-subject marker. Thus:

- Replace the subject marker with a non-subject marker
  *Mahusay **ang** mekaniko.   ... **ng** mekaniko.*
- Replace the affixes of the adjective or verb modifier with *napaka-*
  ***Ma**husay ang mekaniko   **Napaka**husay ng mekaniko.*

*
Masaya ang piknik.   **Napaka**saya ng piknik.
Mabilis mag-isip si Alice.   **Napaka**bilis mag-isip ni Alice.
Impressive magsalita si Ed.   **Napaka**-impressive magsalita ni Ed.*

Exercise

Translate the following using *napaka-*.

Example:
   You are very good to me.
   Napakabait mo sa akin.

1. The typhoon is very strong.

2. The soldier is very cowardly.

3. This one is very stupid.

4. She is very smart.

5. The news is very disgusting.

b. Think of five situations in your or somebody else's life worthy of being expressed in the intensive.

1.

2.

3.

4.

5.

The Existential Sentence

May / *mayroon* sentences are often identified as existential sentences. Existentials express:

- the existence of something:
  May *Diyos.*   God exists; or, There is God.
- the existence of something somewhere:
  May *giyera sa Asya.*   There is war in Asia.
- the existence of something owned or possessed:
  Mayroon *siyang pera.* He has money.

Mayroon is a combination of *may* and *roon*, the latter being a locative demonstrative. *Wala* is the negative form of *may* / *mayroon*. It means non-possession or non-existence.

> **Walang** *Diyos.*   There is no God.
> **Walang** *giyera sa Asya.* There is no war in Asia.
> **Wala** *siyang pera.*   He has no money

Exercise

Negate the following existentials using *wala.*

Example: *May anak si Mindi.*   ***Walang anak si Mindi.***

1. *May puno sa garden.*
2. *May kinabukasan si Inigo.*
3. *May pakpak ang balita.*
4. *May tenga ang lupa.*
5. *May amoy ang sandwits.*

May is always followed immediately by the object phrase. With *mayroon*, the object phrase may occur before or after the possessor.

> *May alipunga si Alberto.*
> *May **masamang** alipunga si Alberto.*
> **May **si Albertong** alipunga.*   (Why is this sentence incorrect?)
> *Mayroong alipunga si Alberto.*
> *Mayroon si Albertong alipunga.*

The possessor is always an *ang* phrase.

> May konsiyensiya *ang* Gobernador.
> May konsiyensiya **ng* Gobernador.

Exercise

Answer the following questions with *mayroon* or *wala* sentences.

Example:
May tiket ka ba?	**Wala, wala akong tiket.**
	Oo, mayroon akong tiket.

1. *May nakaupo ba dito?*
2. *May mga silya ba sa kuwarto?*
3. *May susi ka ba?*
4. *May barya ba kayo?*
5. *May anak na ba kayo?*
6. *May sigarilyo ka ba?*
7. *May hinihintay ka ba?*
8. *May gagawin ka ba?*
9. *May kasalanan ba siya?*
10. *May ibibigay ba ako sa iyo?*
11. *May uuwian ka ba sa Pasko?*
12. *May itatanong daw ba siya sa iyo?*
13. *May sasabihin ba si Perla sa akin?*
14. *May pangako ba ako sa iyo?*
15. *May tatakbuhan ka ba sa kagipitan?*

When the existential expresses the existence of something in some location, it is subjectless.

> *May tao sa silong.*
> *May yelo sa bundok.*
> *May ulap sa langit.*

When it expresses the existence of something owned or possessed, it has a subject, which is the possessor.

> *May libro si **Carol**.*
> *May kalukohan **si Tarcila**.*
> *May sira **ang bahay**.*

When the object whose existence is asserted is a nominalized verb, the existential may or may not have a subject depending on the focus of the verb. An actor focus verb requires no subject, whereas an object focus verb requires a subject.

> *May bumili ng saging.*   (Actor-focus verb has no subject.)
> *May kumuha ng pera.*
> *May nagdala ng kape.*

> *May biniling mangga **si Dante**.*   (Object-focus verb has a subject.)
> *May kinuhang kahon **ang babae**.*
> *May kapeng dinala **si Marsha**.*

Exercises

a. Add *sa* phrases or *ang* phrases or both where appropriate.

Example:
  May libro   **May libro sa mesa.** (without subject)
                 May libro ang bata. (with subject)

1. *May pera*
2. *May langgam*
3. *May idea*
4. *May salubsob*
5. *May hinanakit*

b. Supply subject and object phrases to the following existential sentences.

1. *May ininom na*
2. *May itinapong*
3. *May nawalang*
4. *May biniling*
5. *May sinandok na*

chapter 3

The Verb: Aspect and Focus

Aspect and **focus** are two very important properties of the verb. Aspect refers to the expression of duration in the verb, and focus to the expression in the verb of the role of the subject or primary participant in the action. A good understanding of these two features will help eliminate a great deal of the errors that plague the learner.

Aspect

Aspect indicates, by means of verbal inflection, whether the action has been started or not, and if started, whether it has been completed or if it is still continuing. Verbal inflection includes affixation and/or reduplication. Reduplication is the repetition of parts of the affix or of the root.

The three aspects of the verbs are:

- **completed**, for action started and terminated,
- **contemplated**, for action not started,
- **incompleted**, for action started but not yet completed or action still in progress.

The form of the verb that does not imply any aspect is the **neutral** or **infinitive** form. *Ka-* verbs, discussed earlier, are sometimes considered to form another aspect category, referred to as **recent perfective.**

The closest equivalent in English to the completed aspect is the past tense, to the contemplated aspect the future tense, and to the incompleted aspect the progressive.

47

Verbal inflection to indicate aspect differs according to the affix class of the verb. The four verb affix classes are -um-, mag-, ma-, and mang-.

The -um- Verb

The neutral or infinitive form of the -um- verb is constructed by placing -um- before the first vowel of the verb or base. The completed aspect is similarly formed.

Root	*langoy*	to swim
	alis	to go away
Neutral	**lum**angoy	(-um- inserted before first vowel of root)
	umalis	
Completed	**lum**angoy	(-um- inserted before first vowel of root)
	umalis	

The contemplated aspect is formed by reduplicating the first consonant and vowel of the root, or simply the vowel in roots that begin with a vowel.

Contemplated	**la**langoy	(The first CV or first V of root is
	aalis	reduplicated)

In the incompleted aspect, the first (consonant)-vowel of the root is reduplicated, and then the affix -um- is inserted before the first vowel of the reduplicated base.

Incompleted	**lum**alangoy	(-um- is inserted in the duplicate syllable)
	umaalis	

Here are more examples:

Root	Neutral / Completed	Contemplated	Incompleted
ulan	umulan	uulan	umuulan
takbo	tumakbo	tatakbo	tumatakbo
tanggi	tumanggi	tatanggi	tumatanggi
yakap	yumakap	yayakap	yumayakap
salubong	sumalubong	sasalubong	sumasalubong
wagayway	wumagayway	wawagayway	wumawagayway
lapit	lumapit	lalapit	lumalapit

Exercises

a. Attach -*um*- to the following roots.

1. *hiram*   **humiram**   6. *kain*
2. *sayaw*   7. *bilang*
3. *uwi*   8. *pasok*
4. *sama*   9. *labas*
5. *tulong*   10. *iyak*

b. Give the different aspect forms of the following -*um*- verbs.

Neutral	Completed	Contemplated	Incompleted
1. *pumunta*			
2. *bumasa*			
3. *umupo*			
4. *gumising*			

The *mag-* Verb

The neutral form of this class of verbs is constructed by prefixing *mag-* to the verb root.

> Root *laba* to wash
> Neutral form **mag**laba

The completed aspect is formed by changing *m-* of the prefix to *n-* .

> Completed **n**aglaba

The contemplated aspect is formed by reduplicating the first syllable of the root and prefixing *mag-* to the base.

> Contemplated **mag**lalaba

The incompleted aspect is formed by prefixing *nag-* to the verb root and reduplicating its first syllable.

> Incompleted **nag**lalaba

Examples:

Root	Neutral	Completed	Contemplated	Incompleted
dala	magdala	nagdala	magdadala	nagdadala
tanim	magtanim	nagtanim	magtatanim	nagtatanim
tangka	magtangka	nagtangka	magtatangka	nagtatangka
alis	mag-alis	nag-alis	mag-aalis	nag-aalis

Exercise

Give the different aspect forms of the following *mag-* verbs.

	Neutral	Completed	Contemplated	Incompleted
1.	maglinis			
2.	magbigay			
3.	mag-ani			
4.	magsine			
5.	magsauli			
6.	mag-ahit			
7.	magsigarilyo			
8.	mag-umpisa			
9.	mag-aral			
10.	magturo			

The *ma-* Verb

The *ma-* verb follows the same aspect formation as does the *mag-* verb. *N-* replaces the *m-* of the prefix for the started action and the first consonant-vowel or vowel of the root is reduplicated for action not terminated.

Root	tulog	to sleep
Neutral	**ma**tulog	to sleep
Completed	**na**tulog	slept
Incompleted	**na**tutulog	sleeping
Contemplated	**ma**tutulog	will sleep

Exercise

Give the different aspect forms of the following *ma-* verbs.

	Root	Neutral	Completed	Incompleted	Contemplated
1.	*galit*	*magalit*	*nagalit*	*nagagalit*	*magagalit*
2.	*ligo*				
3.	*hulog*				
4.	*takot*				
5.	*kinig*				
6.	*uhaw*				
7.	*gutom*				
8.	*pagod*				
9.	*nood*				
10.	*loko*				

The *mang-* Verb

The *mang-* affix undergoes the same *m-* to *n-* replacement for started action and reduplication for non-terminated action, but there are some changes in the final nasal sound of the affix as it gets influenced by the following initial sound of the root. The first consonant of the root may drop under certain conditions. These changes may be represented by the following rule, where *p, t, k, b,* or *d* are initial sounds of the root or base.

$$mang + \begin{matrix} b \\ p \end{matrix} \quad => \quad mam$$

$$mang + \begin{matrix} t \\ d \end{matrix} \quad => \quad man$$

$$mang + k \quad => \quad mang$$

Examples:

mang + bili	*mamili*
mang + pulot	*mamulot*

mang + tahi	manahi
mang + dalangin	manalangin
mang + sunog	manunog
mang + kuha	manguha

The consonants *h, g,* the semivowels *y* and *w,* and the vowels do not influence the final nasal of the prefix *mang-* to change.

mang + gulo	manggulo
mang + huli	manghuli
mang + yakap	mangyakap
mang + wasak	mangwasak
mang + asar	mang-asar
mang + inis	mang-inis
mang + umit	mang-umit

After the affixed verb form has undergone changes, the second syllable is reduplicated to form the incompleted and completed forms.

Neutral	mamili
Completed	namili
Contemplated	mamimili
Incompleted	namimili

Where no changes occur, the first syllable of the root is reduplicated.

Neutral	manggulo
Completed	nanggulo
Contemplated	manggugulo
Incompleted	nanggugulo

Exercise

Give the different aspect forms of the following *mang-* verbs.

		Neutral	Completed	Contemplated	Incompleted
1.	hiram				
2.	kailangan				
3.	pulot				
4.	budbud				
5.	bigay				
6.	abala				

7. *suntok*
8. *itlog*
9. *sungkit*
10. *gulo*

Verb bases having initial consonants *l* and a few with *d* retain these sounds after the final nasal of *mang-* has undergone the sound change.

mang	+ likum	manlikum
mang	+ loko	manloko
mang	+ lito	manlito
mang	+ dagok	mandagok
mang	+ daya	mandaya
mang	+ dukot	mandukot
mang	+ dukit	mandukit
mang	+ damo	mandamo
mang	+ dakma	mandakma

Focus

Focus is the expression in the verb of the grammatical role of the subject of the sentence. The role can be one of actor, object, benefactor, location, instrument, or cause. As in Aspect, this expression is in the form of verbal affixes. Different roles induce different affixes on the verb.

When the subject performs the role of an actor, the verb is in actor focus; when the subject of the sentence is an object, the verb is in object focus, and so forth. Thus, in addition to these two focuses, the verb may be in benefactor focus, locative focus, instrumental focus, or causative focus.

Focus is similar to *voice*, except that in Tagalog, as shown above, the division would not be limited to the English active (actor) and passive (object) voices.

Actor Focus

The verbal affixes that indicate that the actor, doer, or the originator of the action is in focus are *-um-*, *mag-*, *mang-*, and *ma-*.

Verb Affix	Verb	Subject	Object
-um-	Gumawa	ang panadero	ng tinapay.
	The baker made some bread.		
mag-	Magbili	ka	ng gulay.
	(You) sell some vegetables.		
mang-	Manghuli	kayo	ng daga.
	You catch some mice.		
ma-	Matulog	na kayo.	
	You sleep.		

As observed earlier, each of these focus affixes follow unique ways of inflecting for aspect.

Exercises

a. Supply the missing words.

1. *(bili+um)*   *siya ng damit.* (Answer: *bumili)*

2. *Nagtapon si Esmeralda*   *basura sa labas.*

3. *Nahulog*   *Roberto sa hagdanan.*

4. *(kuha+um)*   *ang nanay ng pera sa alkansya.*

5. *(mang+bili)*   *sila ng regalo sa Sears.*

b. Construct the following into actor focus sentences. Supply the missing affixes and particles.

Example:
upo, Herminigildo, bangko
Umupo **si** Herminigildo **sa** bangko.

1. *tapon, ako, basura*

2. *inom, Daniel, serbesa, tindahan*

3. *luto, Nanay, pansit*

4. *basa, estudyante, sulat*

5. *sauli, siya, libro, laybrari*

Object or Goal Focus

Verbal affixes that indicate that the subject of the sentence is the object or goal of the action include the suffixes -*in* and -*an* and the prefix *i-*.

Verb Affix	Verb	Actor	Object (subject)
-*in*	*Pukpukin*	*mo*	*ang pako.*
	(You) hammer the nail.		
-*an*	*Hugasan*	*mo*	*ang kotse.*
	(You) wash the car.		
i-	*Isulat*	*mo*	*ang kuwento.*
	(You) write the story.		

The -*in* Object-Focus Suffix The neutral form of the -*in* verb is formed by suffixing -*in* to the verb root.

Neutral	*alis* + **in**	*alisin*
	basa + **in**	*basahin*

If the root ends in a vowel, -*hin* is suffixed to the root rather than -*in*. With the addition of the suffix -*in* there is also a shift in stress to the next syllable toward the end of the word.

The completed aspect is formed by placing -*in* before the first vowel of the root.

Completed	**in** + *alis*	*inalis*
	in + *basa*	*binasa*

Exercise

Construct the neutral and completed aspect of the following roots.

	Roots	Neutral	Completed
1.	buhat		
2.	kuha	kunin*	
3.	hingi		
4.	kopya		
5.	bura		

*Note: *kunin* is an irregular form.

In the incompleted aspect, the first syllable of the root is reduplicated and then the infix is inserted before the first vowel of the base.

Incompleted	*in + alis*	*in + basa*	
	aalis	**ba**basa	(Reduplicate first consonant-vowel,
	inaalis	bi**na**basa	then insert -*in*- before first vowel)

The contemplated aspect is similar to the neutral form but with the first syllable of the base reduplicated.

Contemplated	*in + alis*	*in + basa*	
	alis**in**	basa**hin**	(Attach -*in* at end of root,
	aalisin	**ba**basahin	then reduplicate first consonant-vowel)

Exercise

Construct the incompleted and contemplated aspects of the following -*in* roots and indicate the stress.

Roots	Incompleted	Contemplated
1. ayos		
2. gawa*		
3. punit		
4. tahi*		

*The contemplated forms of these roots are irregular.

The *i*-Object-Focus Prefix The neutral aspect of the *i*-verb is formed by prefixing *i*- to the verb root. To this neutral form, insert the infix -*in*- before the first vowel of the root and the completed aspect is formed. If instead the first (consonant)-vowel of the neutral form is reduplicated, the contemplated aspect is formed. If the first (consonant)-vowel of the neutral form is reduplicated and then the infix -*in*- is inserted before the first vowel of this reduplicated syllable, the incompleted aspect is formed.

Root	*abot*	*tapon*	
Neutral	*iabot*	*itapon*	
Completed	*iniabot**	it**ina**pon	(To the neutral form, insert -*in*- before first vowel of root)
Contemplated	i**a**abot	ita**ta**pon	(Reduplicate first (C)V- of root in the neutral form)
Incompleted	i**nia**abot*	iti**na**tapon	(Reduplicate first (C)V- of root, then insert -*in*- before first vowel of reduplicated syllable)

*Remember from an earlier lesson that the infix -*in*- becomes *ni*- before vowels and the consonants *h, y, n, l.*

Exercise

Construct the different aspects of the following actor focus *i*- verbs.

Neutral	Completed	Contemplated	Incomplete
ibigay	*ibinigay*	*ibibigay*	*ibinibigay*

1. *isauli*
2. *ihagis*
3. *iyari*
4. *ikuha*
5. *ilagay*

Locative Focus

The verbal affixes that indicate that the subject is the location of the action or that the action is done toward that direction include -*in*, -*an*, and *pag...an*.

Locative Affix	Verb	Actor	Locative Subject
-*an*	*Punasan*	*mo*	*ang mesa.*
-*in*	*Balibagin*	*mo*	*ang mangga.*
pag...an	**Pagsabihan**	*mo*	*si Belen.*

-*An* and -*in* follow a consonant sound, and -*han* and -*hin* a vowel sound. There is also an accompanying shift in stress to the next syllable with the addition of the suffix.

	punas + an	balibag + in	pag + sabi + an
Neutral	punas**an**	balibag**in**	**pag**sabihan
Completed	**pin**unasan	**bin**alibag	**pin**agsabihan
Contemplated	**pu**punasan	**ba**balibagin	pag**sa**sabihan
Incomplete	**pinu**punasan	**bina**balibag	**pin**ag**sa**sabihan

A couple of things to note: The locative suffix -*in* is dropped in the completed aspect, and the incompleted aspect infix -*in*- is inserted in the reduplicated CV in both the -*an* and -*in* verbs.

Exercise

Construct the different aspects of the following locative focus verbs.

	Neutral	Completed	Contemplated	Incompleted
1.	*tapunan*			
2.	*hulugan*			
3.	*pagsampayan*			
4.	*kunin**			
5.	*kainan*			
6.	*pagsaingan*			

kunin is from *kuha* + *in.*

If the verb has a directional meaning, for example, *balibag* 'throw something at,' the focus of the verb is sometimes referred to as "source" or "goal" depending on the direction of the action.

Benefactive Focus

The verbal affixes that indicate that the beneficiary of the action is the subject are generally *i-* or *ipag-*.

	Verb	Actor	Beneficiary-Subject	Goal/Object
i-	*Ibili*	*mo*	*ang Nanay*	*ng sapatos.*

You buy a pair of shoes for Mother.

	Verb	Actor	Beneficiary-Subject	Goal/Object
ipag-	**Ipag**laba	*mo*	*ang maysakit*	*ng damit.*

You wash clothes for the sick one.

The *ipag-* verbs behave like the *i-* verbs except that the *-in-* or the indicator of the action started is infixed in the prefix rather than in the root.

Neutral	**ipag**luto	**i**bili
Completed	**ipin**agluto	**ibin**ili
Contemplated	**ipagl**uluto	**ibib**ili
Incompleted	**ipin**agluluto	**ibin**ibili

Exercise

Form the different aspects of the following verbs.

	Neutral	Completed	Contemplated	Incompleted
1.	ipaglaba			
2.	ipaglinis			
3.	ipaghanda			
4.	ipagdala			
5.	ipagpinta			
6.	ilabas			
7.	ikuha			
8.	ikopya			
9.	isulat			
10.	ihingi			

Instrumental Focus

The verbal affix that refers to anything used or acted upon to bring about the action as subject is *ipang-*, usually shortened to *i-*.

	Verb	Actor	Instrument-Subject	Goal
ipang-	**Ipang**hiwa	mo	ang kutsilyo	ng mangga.

You use the knife to cut the mango.

The *ipang-*verb is inflected in the same manner as the *ipag-* verb. In addition, its final nasal undergoes the same sound changes *mang-* undergoes.

	ipang + tahi
Neutral	**ipang***tahi*, **ipan***ahi*
Completed	*ipinangtahi*, *ipinanahi*
Contemplated	*ipangtatahi*, *ipananahi*
Incompleted	*ipinangtatahi*, *ipinananahi*

Exercises

A. Form the different aspects of the following *ipang-* verbs.

Root	Neutral	Completed	Contemplated	Incompleted
1. *kuha*				
2. *sandok*				
3. *linis*				
4. *hiwa*				
5. *hakot*				

B. Change the following sentences into different types of focus as cued.
OF = object focus, BF = benefactive focus, LF = locative focus

1. *Kumuha siya ng litrato sa album para kay Helen.*
a. -in   (OF)   *Kinuha niya ang litrato sa album para kay Helen.*
b. -an   (LF)
c. i-   (BF)

2. *Bibili ang drayber ng gasolina sa gasolinahan para sa kanyang diyep.*
a. -in   (OF)
b. -an   (LF)
c. i-   (BF)

3. *Naglalagay sila ng pagkain sa mga pinggan para sa mga pulis tuwing tanghali.*
a. i-   (OF)
b. -an   (LF)
c. ipag- (BF)

4. *Humingi ka ng pera sa Tatay para sa akin.*
a. -in   (OF)
b. -an   (LF)
c. i-   (BF)

5. *Naglaba si Maria ng medyas sa lababo para sa anak niya noong Sabado.*

a. *-an* (OF)

b. *pag-...-an* (LF)

c. *ipag-* (BF)

C. Change the focus of the following sentences as cued by the *ang* phrases and then change the same sentence into other possible types of focus.

1. *(bili) niya ng tela **ang tindahan ni Aling Nena** para sa akin.*

a.

b.

c.

d.

2. *(tapon) ng tatay **ang basura** sa ilog.*

a.

b.

3. *(kuha) ng nars ang tubig **ang pasiyente niya.***

a.

b.

4. *(inom) niya ng gatas **ang aking baso.***

a.

b.

5. *(hiram) ko **ang bisikleta** para sa kaniya.*

a.

b.

6. *(sauli) ko **siya** ng libro sa laybrari.*

a.

b.

c.

7. *(drayb)* **ako** *para sa lola ko.*

a.

8. *(upo)* *ko* **ang bagong** *silya.*

a.

b.

9. *(huli)* **si Damian** *ng isda sa sapa para kay Anita.*

a.

b.

c.

d.

10. *(isip)* **si Salvador** *ng sagot.*

a.

b.

chapter 4

Simple Expansions
of the Basic Sentence

There are three simple ways to expand a basic sentence: identify other participants in the event; modify the event or the noun participants; and compound the event, the participants, or the modifiers.

Identifying Other Participants

One way to expand a simple sentence is to identify the other participants in the event, where appropriate. We typically only report the actor and the object, making assumptions that the other participants are either understood or inconsequential. In addition to the actor and object participants, noun phrases may perform the roles of location, beneficiary, or instrument. Here's a sentence that includes all five participants.

> *Binasag* (**verb**, broken)
>   *ni Sandro* (**actor**, by Sandro)
>   *sa kusina* (**location**, in the kitchen)
>   *ang alkansya* (**object**, the piggybank)
>   *para kay Dan* (**benefactor**, for Dan)
>   *sa pamamagitan ng martilyo.* (**instrumental**, with a hammer)

As shown earlier, one of the participants is focused as the subject or topic of the sentence; in the above example, this is *alkansya*. The subject word is introduced or marked by *ang* or *si*. When not functioning as subject, these phrases retain their own markings:

63

64 Simple Expansions

Non-Subject Noun Markers		
Role	Personal	Non-Personal
actor	*ni*	*ng*
goal	*ni*	*ng*
location	*kay*	*sa*
beneficiary	*para kay*	*para sa*
instrument	*sa pamamagitan ni*	*sa pamamagitan ng*

Based on their markers, these phrases are grouped into two: those marked by *ni* and *ng*, called the *ng*-phrases, thus the actor, goal, and instrument phrases; and those marked by *kay* and *sa*, called the *sa*-phrases, which include the location and beneficiary phrases.

Exercises

a. Supply the missing markers.

1. *Kumuha ang kahera*   *barya.*

2. *Nagpinta siya*   *bahay.*

3. *Pumasyal sila*   *tabing-dagat.*

4. *Natulog sina Pete*   *sala.*

5. *Naghanap ang ninang*   *regalo*   *inaanak niya.*

6. *Nahulog ang bata*   *sahig.*

7. *Nagdeposito si Mrs. Lopez*   *pera*   *bangko.*

8. *Tumayo ang ang artista*   *entablado.*

9. *Bumili ka ng selyo*   *Joaquin.*

10. *Pinitas*   *Damian*   *saging.*

b. Identify the role of the phrases you supplied with markers in Exercise *a*.

Phrase	Role
1. *ng barya*	*goal*

The *ng* and *sa*-phrases have pronoun and demonstrative counterparts. The following chart also gives the *ang* set that marks the subject of the sentence.

Noun Markers

		Non-Subject		Subject
Non-Personal	**(sg.)**	*ng*	*sa*	*ang*
	(pl.)	*ng mga*	*sa mga*	*ang mga*
Personal	**(sg.)**	*ni*	*kay*	*si*
	(pl.)	*nina*	*kina*	*sina*

sg. = singular; **pl.** = plural

Pronouns

	Person		Non-Subject		Subject
(sg.)	1		*ko*	*(sa) akin*	*ako*
	2		*mo*	*(sa) iyo*	*ikaw, ka*
	3		*niya*	*(sa) kaniya*	*siya*
(pl.)	1	**inclusive**	*namin*	*(sa) amin*	*kami*
		exclusive	*natin*	*(sa) atin*	*tayo*
	2		*ninyo*	*(sa) inyo*	*kayo*
	3		*nila*	*(sa) kanila*	*sila*

Demonstratives

	Non-Subject		Subject
Object near speaker	*nito*	*dito*	*ito*
Object near listener	*niyan*	*diyan*	*iyan*
Object away from speaker and listener	*niyon*	*doon*	*iyon*

Exercises

c. Substitute pronouns or demonstratives for the phrases in
    Exercise **a.**

1. *ng barya*   *nito*

d. Add phrases to the following sentences as cued.

1. *Tumalon ang pusa*   (location)
2. *Humingi ang anak niya*   (goal)
3. *Humiram siya*   (goal)   (location)
        (beneficiary).
4. *Nagtapon sila*   (goal)   (location).
        (beneficiary)   (instrument).

e. Supply actor, goal, and location phrases.

	Actor	**Goal**	**Location**
1. *Kumuha*			
2. *Niluto*			
3. *Binasa*			
4. *Kinainan*			
5. *Nagdala*			

Expansion by Modification

Noun Modification

Single-Word Modifiers   Adjectives serve as single-word modifiers of
nouns. They may occur before or after the noun. This modification is made
clear not only by the juxtaposition of the adjective and noun, but also by the
linking of the two words using the linker *na / -ng*. The linker *-ng* is attached

to the first word if it ends in a vowel, or the linker -*g* is attached to if it ends in -*n*. The linker *na* occurs when the word before it ends in a consonant.

adjective + linker + noun	noun + linker + adjective
luma**ng** libro	libro**ng** luma
paling **na** linya	kala**ng** bago
mabait **na** bata	gulong **na** malambot
sapin **na** makapal	supot **na** malaki

Exercise

Supply the correct form of the linker: *na*, -*ng*, or -*g*.

1. maputik   sahig   sahig   maputik
2. maganda   kapalaran   kapalaran   maganda
3. masama   kaibigan   kaibigan   masama
4. mahal   na kotse   kotse   mahal
5. malakas   hangin   hangin   malakas

Phrase Modifiers   Phrases may be used to modify nouns. Like single-word modifiers, phrase modifiers may occur before or after the noun modified. As well, the modifier and the noun are linked by some form of the nasal linker depending on the last sound of the first word (see above for the rule). Locative, possessive, benefactive, and informational phrases are some of the kinds of phrases that may be used as noun modifiers.

	Phrase Modifier	Noun	Phrase Modifier
locative	ang nasa kusina**ng**	bisita	
		ang bisita**ng**	nasa kusina
possessive	ang kay Pedro**ng**	libro	
		ang libro*	ni Pedro
benefactive	ang para sa bata**ng**	libro	
		ang libro**ng**	para sa bata
informational	ang tungkol kay Fe **na**	libro	
		ang libro**ng**	tungkol kay Fe

*Note the absence of the linker before the possessor phrase *ni Pedro*.

Exercise

a. Give another way of constructing the following modification structures.

Example: *ang malapit nang malusaw na yelo*
           ang yelong malapit nang malusaw

1. *ang nasa ibabaw ng piyano na libro*
2. *ang taong nasa tabi ng simbahan*
3. *ang para sa karterong bisikleta*
4. *ang tungkol sa kaniyang balita*
5. *ang bahay ng kapatid ko*

b. List the nouns described in the above constructions. In the example, this is the noun *yelo*.

1.   2.   3.   4.   5.

Naka-Constructions as Modifiers   *Naka-* is an adjective prefix which can be followed by nouns (limited to things or accessories that can be worn or put on) and by verb roots.

ang babaing nakaluksa	the woman (who is) in mourning
ang babaing naka-asul	the woman (who is) in blue
ang babaing nakakimona	the woman (who is) wearing a *kimona*
ang lalaking nakatayo	the man (who is) standing
ang lalaking nakangiti	the man (who is) smiling

Exercise

Supply the *naka-* constructions describing the nouns.

1. *ang babaing **naka-asul***   (in blue)

                                       (in uniform)

                                       (in mourning)

                                       (wearing a jacket)

2. *ang sekretaryang*	(standing by the door)
	(sitting on the stairs)
	(looking at you)
	(smiling at us)
	(riding in a car)

Taga-Constructions as Modifiers   *Taga-*, a prefix that occurs before nouns, also occurs before verb roots to mean "one whose occupation, work, or duty is the one expressed by the verb."

*ang sundalong **taga**linis ng baril*	*linis* 'clean'
*ang babaing **taga**bili ng pagkain*	*bili* 'buy'
*ang binatilyong **taga**kuha ng gamot*	*kuha* 'get'

Exercise

Complete the following sentences with *taga-*modifiers indicating usual occupation or activity.

Nagkasakit ang dalagang...

1. *(luto ng pagkain)* **tagaluto ng pagkain**
2. *(laba ng damit)*
3. *(tanggap ng bisita)*
4. *(sagot ng mga sulat)*
5. *(makinilya ng leksyon)*

Verbal Constructions as Modifiers   Verbs can be used as the basis of a modification structure after nouns.

*Ang batang **umiiyak**...*	The child (who is) crying...
*Ang pasyenteng **naglalakad**...*	The patient (who is) walking...
*Ang tanod na **nakaupo** sa lilim*	The guard (who is) sitting in the shade...
*Ang nars na **gumamot** kay Don...*	The nurse (who) treated Don...

Exercises

a. Use the supplied verbs as modifiers of the preceding nouns.

1. *ang isdang (palag)*   **ang isdang pumapalag**
2. *ang pulis na (galit)*
3. *mga matang (ngiti)*
4. *ilong na (simangot)*
5. *mga paang (sayaw)*
6. *ang hardinerong (dilig) ng halaman*
7. *ang babysitter na (alaga) ng bata*
8. *ang karpinterong (gawa) ng kabinet*
9. *ang kusinerong (tikim) ng pansit*
10. *ang tinderang (tinda) sa palengke*

b. Expand the following sentences by adding the supplied words and phrases as modifiers.

Example:
*Nasunog ang **bahay**. (bago, malaki, nina Alice at Dan)*
*Nasunog ang **bago** at **malaking** bahay **nina Alice at Dan**.*

1. *Ipinagbili ni Alberto ang **stereo**.*   *(luma, walang-kuwenta, ni Nora)*
2. *Pinakinggan ni Dan ang **concerto**.*   *(popular, sa byulin, ni Brahms)*
3. *Binasa ng klase ang **kuwento**.*   *(malalim, hindi-maintindihan, ni Willie)*
4. *Isinara ang **pinto**.*   *(malaki, mabigat, umiingit)*
5. *Nakipag-away si Fe sa **drayber**.*   *(bastos, walang-modo, ng diyep)*

Modification structures involving adjective and phrase modifiers can be given a complex structure analysis where the modifiers represent an embedded sentence. Verbal construction modifiers as embedded sentences are discussed in some detail in a later section.

Verbal Modification

Except for adverbs indicating time or duration of time, verbal modification is marked by the occurrence of the linker *na* / *-ng* between the modifier and the verb or by the adverbial marker *nang* when the modifier follows the verb.

Ma- Modifiers   A limited number of combinations of *ma-* and a base word are used to modify the verb. They function like adverbs of manner. The verbs occurring after these adjectives are in the infinitive form (i.e., uninflected for aspect).

ma- modifier	linker	infinitive verb	subject
Madalas	(na)	*magsimba*	*si Lolita.*
Marunong	(na)	*magtrabaho*	*si Dante.*
Madali	-ng	*matuto*	*si Tarcila.*

The linker *na* in this contruction is often dropped, but not the linker *-ng.*

Exercise

Add linkers (*na* / *-ng*) where necessary.

1. *Malimit*   *linisin ang bahay ni Martha.*
2. *Masama*   *magtapon ng asin.*
3. *Matagal*   *ibili si Mario ng sapatos.*
4. *Mabagal*   *kumilis si Damian.*
5. *Madalang*   *kumanta si Ramon.*

Verbal Modifiers   Verbal forms may modify verbs; both the verbal modifier and the modified verb usually have the same focus. These verbal modifiers are often in the incompleted aspect form.

Verbal Modifier	Verb		
Umiiyak na	*umalis*	*si Susan.*	Susan left crying.
Humihikbing	*natulog*	*si Juliet.*	Juliet slept sobbing.
Umuubong	*nagsalita ang sigarero.*		(lit.) The smoker talked coughing.
Nag-iisip na	*umupo*	*ang senador.*	(lit.) The senator sat down thinking.

Intensified Modifiers   Modifiers of verbs may be intensified by reduplication or by the addition of adverbial intensifiers to the modifier.

(+ *ubod*)	*Tumakbo siya nang* **ubod** *nang bilis.* He ran very fast.
(+ *napaka-*)	*Tumawa siya nang* **napaka**lakas. He laughed very loudly.
(+ base reduplication)	*Lumakad siya nang* **dahan**-*dahan.* He walked very slowly.
(+ base reduplication and linker)	*Nagbihis siya nang* **magandang**-*maganda.* She dressed very beautifully.
(+ *pagka-* and base reduplication)	*Umiyak siya nang* **pagkalakas**-*lakas.* He cried very loudly.

Exercise

Intensify the verbal modifiers in the following sentences as cued.

1. *Lumakad siya nang mabilis* (+ *ubod*).
2. *Kumanta siya nang maganda* (+ *napaka-*).
3. *Kumilos siya nang marahan* (*pagka-* + base reduplication).
4. *Tumugtog siya nang mahusay* (+ base reduplication and linker).
5. *Sumigaw siya nang malakas* (+ base reduplication).

Modifying the Single-Word Modifier

Persons, things, and actions may be compared in terms of degrees of equality, superiority, or inferiority. These degrees of comparison are indicated by comparative markers.

	Comparative Markers
Equality	*magkasing-, kasing-*
Non-Equality	*mas, sa/kaysa (sa), (kaysa) kay*
Superlative	*pinaka-*

Equality   To express the same degree of equality in nouns or verbs being compared, the adjective root is prefixed by *magkasing-* or *kasing-*.

> **Magkasing***taas si Karla at si Frank (sina Karla at Frank).*
> **Magkasing***bilis silang tumakbo sa kusina.*
> **Magkasing***bagsik ang mga aso natin.*

Exercise

Combine the following sentences using *magkasing-*.

1. *Maputi si Lydia. Maputi rin si Mary.*
   Magkasingputi sina Lydia at Mary.
2. *Matamis ang papaya. Matamis rin ang saging.*

3. *Maikli ang pasensiya ko. Maikli rin ang pasensiya niya.*

4. *Tuso* (shrewd) *si Brian. Tuso rin si John.*

5. *Madulas ang dila ni Efren. Madulas din ang dila ni Ramona.*

With *kasing-* as the comparative marker, the two nouns compared have different markers. The noun that functions as the standard is marked with *ng*; the noun that is being compared to the standard is marked by the subject marker *ang*.

> **Kasing***galing* **ng** *Presidente* **ang** *senador.*
> **Kasing***bagal* **ni** *Nena* **si** *Lily.*
> **Kasing***bilis tumakbo* **ni** *Ben* **si** *Carl.*
> **Kasing***lapad ng ngiti ni Amado* **ang** *kanyang noo.*

Exercise

Use *kasing-* instead of *magkasing-* for sentences in the previous exercise.

1.

2.

3.

4.

5.

Non-Equality   When the quality in one noun being compared is more than the quality in the other, the phrase markers *kaysa kay* or *kaysa sa* occur before the personal or non-personal noun being compared. The adjective is marked by *mas, lalo,* or *higit na.*

> **Mas** *malakas si Jaime* **kaysa kay** *Johnny.*
> **Lalong** *matibay ang Volks* **kaysa sa** *Fiat.*
> **Higit na** *mabagal tumakbo ang kalesa* **kaysa** *karetela.*

Mas is more common; *higit* is on the formal side. *Kay* or *sa* may be omitted, leaving behind *kaysa.*

Exercise

Use *mas* and *kaysa sa* or *kaysa kay* in answering the following questions.

1. *Alin ang mas mahal, ang* Volks *o ang* Cadillac?

2. *Alin ang mas maasim, ang dalanghita o ang manggang hilaw?*

3. *Alin ang mas malamig, ang* Alaska *o ang* New York?

4. *Alin ang mas mahusay, ang* Macintosh computer *o ang* IBM PC?

Superlative Degree   The superlative degree of the adjective is expressed by the affix *pinaka-* prefixed to the *ma-* adjectives or to the adjective roots that do not need the *ma-* affix.

maganda	**pinaka***maganda*
popular	**pinaka***popular*
mura	**pinaka***mura*
mainit	**pinaka***mainit*

The superlative adjective usually occurs before the modified noun.

> *Pinakamagandang artista siya.*
> *Sino ang pinakamagandang artista?*
> *Pinakamagaling na titser si Lydia.*

But, to emphasize the modified noun, the order is reversed.

> *Artista siyang pinakamaganda.*
> *Titser na pinakamagaling si Rhonda.*

Exercises

a. Answer the following questions.

1. *Ano ang pinakamataas na bundok sa buong mundo?*
   Ang Mount Everest ang pinakamataas na bundok .
2. *Sino ang pinakakilalang presidente ng Amerika?*

3. *Ano ang pinakamataas na bundok sa buong mundo?*

4. *Alin ang pinakamaliit na planeta sa solar system?*

5. *Ano ang pinakamalalim na dagat sa mundo?*

6. *Sino ang pinakamahusay na manlalaro ng tenis sa mundo?*

7. *Ayon kay Ripley, aling sili ang pinakamaanghang sa mundo?*

8. *Sino kaya ang pinakamayamang tao sa mundo?*

9. *Alin ang pinakamalaking bansa sa mundo?*

10. *Ano ang pinakamatigas na bato sa mundo?*

b. Construct descriptive, comparative, and superlative sentences using the supplied adjectives, with the corresponding nouns. The first set is done as an example.

1. adjectives   *mabilis / mabagal*
   nouns   *tren, kotse, kalesa*
   a. descriptive   *Mabilis ang tren.*

b.	comparative	*Mas mabilis ang tren kaysa kotse.*
c.	superlative	*Pinakamabilis ang tren.*
d.	superlative	*Pinakamabagal ang kalesa.*

2. adjectives — *mahirap / madali*
   nouns — Science, Math, English
   a. descriptive
   b. comparative
   c. superlative
   d. superlative

3. adjectives — *mabigat / magaan*
   nouns — *tanso, bakal, tingga*
   a. descriptive
   b. comparative
   c. superlative
   d. superlative

4. adjectives — *malamig / mainit*
   nouns — *Amerika, Alaska, Aprika*
   a. descriptive
   b. comparative
   c. superlative
   d. superlative

5. adjectives — *mahal / mura*
   nouns — *ginto, pilak, tanso*
   a. descriptive
   b. comparative
   c. superlative
   d. superlative

Intensified Adjectives   To express high intensity of the quality, the adjective roots are preceded by the following:

Adjective Intensifiers

sukdulan nang	*sukdulan nang ganda*
ubod nang	*ubod nang ganda*
napaka-	*napakaganda*

Exercise

Intensify the descriptive quality expressed in the following sentences.

1. *Mahirap ang Kalkyulus.*
2. *Mahal ang kotse.*
3. *Malamig sa Alaska.*
4. *Mainit sa Aprika.*
5. *Mabigat ang loob ni Jasmine.*

The high intensity of the quality is also expressed when the adjectives are repeated, the two being joined by a linker.

> *magaling **na** magaling*
> *magandang-maganda*
> *pangit **na** pangit*
> *bagung-bago*

Exercise

Intensify the sentences in the previous exercise by repeating the adjectives and joining the repeated forms with the proper form of the linker.

1.
2.
3.
4.
5.

Expansion by Compounding

Two or more syntactically equivalent units can be joined in a coordinate structure by the use of conjunctors. These conjunctions may occur between words, phrases, or sentences. Sentential conjunction is presented in a later chapter.

Conjunctors

at	and
ni...ni	neither...nor
pero, subali't, nguni't, datapwa't	but

Examples:

*ikaw **at** ako*	you and I
*itim **at** puti*	black and white
*aso **at** pusa*	dog and cat
*lumundag **at** tumakbo*	jump and run
*mayaman, tanyag, **at** mabait*	rich, famous, and good
*ikaw **o** ako*	you or I
***ni** ikaw **ni** ako*	neither you nor I
*tanyag **pero** walang-kapararakan*	famous but worthless
*ang bata **at** ang matanda*	the young and the old
*ang buhay mo **o** ang salapi mo*	your life or your money

Events, participants, and modifiers may be compounded.

Compound Events
***Lumundag** at **kumokak** ang palaka.*
***Pumikit** at **kumindat** ang mama.*

Compound Participants

*Lumangoy sina **Pete** at **Abra**.*	(compound actors)
*Itinago ni Debby and **sulat** at ang **telegrama**.*	(compound objects)

Compound Modifiers
*Kumita nang malaki ang **matindi** at **madamdaming** pelikula.*
***Maingat** at **marahang** gumapang and sundalo.*

Exercises

a.   Combine the following sentences by joining the nouns or verbs.

1. *Uminon si Sean. Nagsigarilyo si Sean.*
 Uminon at nagsigarilyo si Sean.
2. *Bumuti si Martin. Lumakas si Martin.*

3. *May sakit si Estefania. May sakit si Ellen.*

4. *Namasyal siya. Nanuod siya ng sine.*

5. *Bumili kami ng hipon. Bumili kami ng isda.*

b. Rearrange the following words to form a sentence; supply the conjunctors *at, o,* or *pero* where necessary.

1. *sumayaw kumanta Cecile programa si sa*
   Sumayaw at kumanta si Cecile sa programa.
2. *nag-travel tatay nanay niya ang*
3. *ambisyosa marunong kapatid niya ang*
4. *ngumiti tumawa ang dalagita*
5. *sumaludo tumayo korporal tatlong ang*
6. *makapal magaan ang libro*
7. *uuwi ka ba hindi?*
8. *mahirap masarap may anak ang*
9. *sumikat nga lumubog din agad ang araw*
10. *tutuo ba hindi ang balita?*

chapter 5

Some Changes in the Basic Sentence

Other Types of Sentences

Inverted Sentences

The basic predicate-subject order of Tagalog statements can be reversed. If the subject is shifted to precede the predicate, the inversion marker *ay* is inserted between the two elements.

Regular Order		Inverted Order		
Predicate	**Subject**	**Subject**	*ay*	**Predicate**
Sundalo	*si Ricardo.*	*Si Ricardo*	*ay*	*sundalo.*
Matamis	*ang atis.*	*Ang atis*	*ay*	*matamis.*
Ngumiti	*si Amelia.*	*Si Amelia*	*ay*	*ngumiti.*

Exercises

a. Change the following into *ay* sentences.

1. *Tumapang si Jorge.*

2. *Huminto ang ulan.*

3. *Lumakad na kayo.*

4. *Malalim ang ilog.*

5. *Mag-ingat ka.**

*Use *ikaw* instead of *ka* in sentence-initial position.

81

b. In the following, the predicates consist of more than one phrase.
   Invert the sentences.

Example:
Nagluto sila ng bulanglang.   **Sila ay nagluto ng bulanglang.**

1. *Pumunta sila sa tabing-dagat.*
2. *Humiram si Dan ng libro sa laybrari.*
3. *Naglagay siya ng pagkain sa bintana.*
4. *Nagsindi si Sol ng kandila sa simbahan.*
5. *Bumasa ako ng nobela habang naghihintay ng sasakyan.*

Negative Statements

To convert an affirmative sentence into a negative, the negative particle *hindi*
is placed before it.

Affirmative	**Negative**	
Pilipino si Jorge.	**Hindi** *Pilipino si Jorge.*	Jorge is not a Filipino.
Naupo si Ana.	**Hindi** *naupo si Ana*	Ana didn't sit down.

Exercises

a. Change the following sentences into negatives.

1. *Mainit ang sabaw.*
2. *Naligwak ang inumin.*
3. *Tumirik ang kotse.*
4. *Sumulat si Joaquin.*
5. *Nahinog ang pakwan.*

When the subject is a pronoun, that pronoun is shifted before the predicate
and thus follows *hindi.*

Abala siya.   **Hindi siya** *abala.*   He is not busy.

b. Convert the following sentences into negatives.

1. *Masuwerte sila.*

2. *Lansones iyan.*

3. *Dalandan ito.*

4. *Nakatulog ako.*

5. *Nag-iisip kayo.*

In the inverted order, *hindi* always follows *ay* and precedes the predicate.

Subject			Predicate
Si Jorge	*ay*	**hindi**	*Pilipino.*
Ang babae	*ay*	**hindi**	*sumagot.*
Ang salamin	*ay*	**hindi**	*nagsisinungaling.*

c. Rewrite the sentences putting the subject before the predicate.

1. *Hindi malamig ang Pilipinas.*

2. *Hindi siya nakatulog kagabi.*

3. *Hindi maganda ang sinabi niya.*

4. *Hindi mahal ang bigas sa Maynila.*

5. *Hindi gumuho ang mga bahay.*

d. Write five sentences about things that didn't happen this week.

1.

2.

3.

4.

5.

Questions

Yes-No Questions

Yes-no questions are usually formed by inserting the question marker *ba* after the first full word of a sentence. There are affirmative yes-no questions and there are negative yes-no questions. A third type is the tag-question.

	Affirmative Yes-No Question
Abala si Jorge.	*Abala **ba** si Jorge?*
Matipid siya.	*Matipid **ba** siya?*
Tumahol ang aso.	*Tumahol **ba** ang aso?*

However, when the subject is the pronoun *ka* or any one-syllable pronoun, then *ba* follows the pronoun.

Matipid ka.	*Matipid ka **ba**?*
Umuwi ka.	*Umuwi ka **ba**?*

Ba also follows one-syllable particles such as *na* and *pa*.

Umuwi ka na.	*Umuwi ka na **ba**?*
Malakas pa ang ulan.	*Malakas pa **ba** ang ulan?*

Exercise

Change the following statements into yes-no questions.

1. *Pagod ang kargador.*
2. *Mahiyain ang tindera.*
3. *Dumating na ang bisita.*
4. *Naghihintay ang mga tao.*
5. *Umuulan pa.*
6. *Tatayo tayo.*
7. *Umalis na ang bus.*
8. *Magtatanim ang mga bata ng kamote.*
9. *Nagluto sila para sa mga bisita.*
10. *Nagtatrabaho ang asawa niya sa panaderya.*

To construct negative yes-no questions, *ba* is inserted after *hindi* in negative statements.

	Negative Yes-No Question
Matulungin si George.	**Hindi ba** *matulungin si George?*
Tumahol ang aso.	**Hindi ba** *tumahol ang aso?*
Interesting ang libro.	**Hindi ba** *interesting ang libro?*

The single-syllable pronoun *ka* precedes *ba* but pronouns having more than one syllable must follow *ba*.

Hindi **ba siya** *aalis?*
Hindi **ka ba** *aalis?*

Exercise

Change the following statements into negative yes-no questions.

1. *Berde ang damo.*
2. *Mabilis ang motorsiklo.*
3. *Maraming pulo sa Pilipinas.*
4. *Lumigaya si Manuela.*
5. *Nalasing siya.*
6. *Ginutom ka.*
7. *Matapang ang kape.*
8. *Namili sila.*
9. *Maanghang ang sili.*
10. *Nanood sila ng basketbol.*

Tag Questions *Hindi ba* is a negative tag question in Tagalog. In rapid speech, it is reduced to *di ba*.

Statement	**Tag Question**	
Artista siya,	**hindi ba?**	He's an actor, isn't he?
Nars si Fe,	**hindi ba?**	Fe is a nurse, isn't she?
Hindi siya pumunta,	**hindi ba?**	He didn't go, did he?
Pumunta siya,	**hindi ba?**	He went, didn't he?

Unlike in English, there is no affirmative tag question in Tagalog. Usually, negative statements are followed by the tag question *ano*.

Negative Statement	Tag Question	
Hindi Pilipino si Art,	**ano?**	Art isn't a Filipino, is he?
Hindi siya pumunta,	**ano?**	He didn't go, did he?

Exercise

1. Change *Mabigat ang dala ko* into a yes-no question.
2. Change #1 into a negative statement.
3. Change #1 into an *ay* sentence.
4. Change #3 into a question.
5. Change #2 into a negative yes-no question.
6. Add a tag question to #1.

Response Patterns to Yes-No Questions

Affirmative Response

Question	Affirmative Response	
Sundalo ba si Jorge?	*Oo, sundalo si Jorge.*	Yes, Jorge is a soldier.
Pangit ba ang sine?	*Oo, pangit ang sine.*	Yes, the movie was lousy.

Plain *oo* 'yes' can stand for the whole affirmative response. In Tagalog, it is common to agree to a negative comment by saying *oo* followed by the negative statement.

Negative Question	Affirmative Response
Hindi doktor si Jorge, ano?	*Oo, hindi siya doktor.*
	Yes, he isn't a doctor.
Hindi pangit ang sine, ano?	*Oo, hindi pangit ang sine.*
	Yes, the movie wasn't lousy.

In English, of course, a negative response is reinforced by another negative expression, e.g., "No, he isn't a soldier."

Negative Response   In contrast to a negative sentence, the negative response has two occurrences of the particle *hindi.*

Negative Question	**Negative Response**
Hindi siya sundalo, ano?	**Hindi, hindi** *siya sundalo*
	No, he's not a soldier.
Hindi pangit ang sine, ano?	**Hindi, hindi** *pangit ang sine.*
	No, the movie wasn't lousy.

Exercise

Complete the responses below.

1. *Titser ka ba sa* Math?   *Hindi,*

2. *Sumakay ba siya sa bus?*   *Oo,*

3. *Hindi nagbaon si Tessi, ano?*   *Oo,*

4. *Insik si Ben, di ba?*   *Hindi,*

5. *Manunulat ba si George?*   *Oo,*

Questions with Interrogative Words

The common interrogative words are:

sino	who	*alin*	which
ano	what	*ilan*	how many
saan	where	*kangino*	whom
kailan	when	*papaano*	how
bakit	why		

Sino *ang dumating?*
Sino *ang abogado mo?*
Ano *ang gusto mo?*
Alin *ang ayaw mo?*
Ilan *ang babae?*
Saan *ang bahay mo?*
Saan *siya pumunta?*
Saan *naglaba si Magda?*
Kailan *siya dumating?*
Kangino *bumili si Eleanor?*
Bakit *umalis si Dorotea?*
Papaano *nililinis ang isda?*

Exercise

Complete the following questions with interrogative words based on the sentence *Nagdala ng pagkain si Virgilio sa opisina kaninang umaga.*

1. *Sino ang nagdala*

2. *Ano ang dinala*

3. *Saan nagdala*

4. *Kailan nagdala*

Inversion of Interrogative Sentences   To invert a question, the *ang* phrase is shifted to initial position in the sentence, which is followed by the question marker *ba*, the inversion marker *ay*, and then the interrogative word. The question words *sino, ano, alin, ilan,* and *kailan* allow inversion.

> *Ang abogado mo ba ay sino?*
> *Ang pangalan mo ba ay ano?*
> *Ang lapis mo ba ay alin?*
> *Ang babae ba ay ilan?*
> *Ang alis mo ba ay kailan?*

Exercise

Supply the missing interrogative words.

1. _____ (who) *ang nagdala ng saging?*

2. _____ (what) *ang dinala ni Ramon?*

3. _____ (when) *itinanim ni Ramon ang saging?*

4. _____ (where) *itinanim ni Ramon ang saging?*

Commands

Affirmative Commands   Infinitive forms of the verbs are used for commands and the actor is limited to the second person form of the personal pronoun.

Focus	Verb	Pronoun	Complement	
Actor	*Maglinis*	ka/kayo	ng bahay.	You clean the house.
	Kumain	ka/kayo	ng almusal.	You eat breakfast.
	Manghuli	ka/kayo	ng daga.	You catch rats.
Goal	*Kunin*	mo/ninyo	ang damit.	You get the clothes.
	Labhan	mo/ninyo	ang sapatos.	You wash the shoes.
	Itulak	mo/ninyo	ang pinto.	You push the door.

Exercises

a. Supply the correct form of the verb.

1. *(linis) ka ng kusina.*

2. *(kopya) mo ang leksyon.*

3. *(inom) ako ng tubig.*

4. *(upo) si Pete sa mesa.*

5. *(kuha) ninyo ang video sa laybrari.*

b. Translate the following.

1. Write on the board. (actor focus)

2. Buy the book. (object focus)

3. Wash the clothes. (object focus)

4. Sing *Dahil sa Iyo.* (object focus)

5. Cook *adobo.* (actor focus)

Negative Commands   *Huwag* instead of *hindi* is used in negative commands.

Huwag *kang tumayo.*	Don't you (sg.) stand.
Huwag *kayong tumayo.*	Don't you (pl.) stand.

Huwag *mong inumin ang gatas.*	Don't you (sg.) drink the milk.
Huwag *ninyong inumin ang gatas.*	Don't you (pl.) drink the milk.

Note the inversion of the pronoun and the verb in negative commands:

Affirmative command:	**Inumin mo** *ang gatas.*
Negative command:	*Huwag* **mong inumin** *ang gatas.*

Also, note the linker *-ng* on the second pronoun in the negative command.

Exercises

a. Transform the following commands into their negatives.

1. *Lutuin mo ang isda.*
2. *Matulog ka nang maaga.*
3. *Ilagay mo ang pagkain sa mesa.*
4. *Makinig ka sa radyo.*
5. *Hugasan mo ang mansanas.*
6. *Hiramin ninyo ang makinilya.*
7. *Maglaro kayo ng madyong.*
8. *Manood kayo ng sine.*
9. *Uminom ka ng gamot.*
10. *Ibigay mo ang libro sa kanya.*

b. Where applicable, change the commands above into their negatives, at the same time changing the focus from actor to object or object to actor. The first sentence above becomes:

   Huwag kang magluto ng isda.

Requests

The verbal prefix *paki-* and the particle *nga* express a request. The verb stem with *paki-* takes an object as the subject of the sentence. The pronoun as actor is limited to the *mo/ninyo* forms.

Pakiabot mo nga ang libro.	You (sg.) please hand over the book.
Pakiabot nga ninyo ang libro.	You (pl.) please hand over the book.

Note the occurrence of *mo* before *nga* and *ninyo* after *nga*. Requests of this form are usually said with a rising intonation.

Exercises

a. Change the following commands into requests.

1. *Hiwain mo ang gulay.*
2. *Pitpitin mo ang bawang.*
3. *Iprito ninyo ang manok.*
4. *Ilaga mo ang karne.*
5. *Ihawin ninyo ang baboy.*

b. Translate the following requests.

1. Please close the windows.
2. Please help him.
3. Please return your chairs.
4. Please mail this letter for me.
5. Please give this to her.

Exhortations

An exhortation construction expresses a wish that an action takes place. It takes the plural pronoun *tayo* for actor-focus verbs and *natin* for goal-focus verbs. This imperative construction is equivalent to the English construction introduced by "let's."

*Kumanta **tayo**.*	Let's sing.
*Linisin **natin** ang kotse.*	Let's clean the car.

The use of *nga* or *naman* adds a meaning of politeness or mild suggestion to the exhortation.

*Kumain **naman** tayo sa labas.*	Let's (this time) eat out.
*Bumili **nga** tayo ng pop.*	Let's buy pop.

Exercises

a.   Change the following commands into exhortations.

1.   *Maglinis kayo ng bahay.*
2.   *Kunin ninyo ang kahoy.*
3.   *Sinupin mo ang garahe.*
4.   *Kumain ka ng sampalok.*
5.   *Itapon ninyo ang basura.*

b.   Translate the following into Tagalog exhortatives.

1.   Let's go to the movies.
2.   Let's watch the parade.
3.   Let's buy ice cream.
4.   Let's repair the car.
5.   Let's roast the pig.

Uncertainty

Kaya' 'perhaps' indicates uncertainty.

> *Tumawag **kaya'** siya sa amin.*   Perhaps she called my home.

Exercise

Translate the following.

1.   Perhaps they should call a doctor.
2.   Perhaps she should call her mother.
3.   Perhaps we should leave early.
4.   Perhaps you should buy a house.
5.   Perhaps he should look for a new job.

Actually, the use of *nga, kaya* and the plural pronoun is an indirect way of giving a command. The most direct command is sentence 1 below and the most indirect way of giving a command is sentence 4.

1. *Magsaing ka.*   Cook rice.
2. *Magsaing ka nga.*   Please cook rice.
3. *Magsaing na tayo.*   Let's cook rice.
4. *Magsaing na kaya tayo.*   What if we cooked rice now?
                               Perhaps we should cook rice now.

Exercise

Change the following direct commands into indirect commands.

Example:
Direct Command: *Hiwain mo ang gulay.*
Indirect Commands: *Hiwain mo nga ang gulay.*
                      Hiwain natin ang gulay.
                      Hiwain kaya natin ang gulay.

1. *Dalhin mo ang libro.*

2. *Bumili ka ng pagkain.*

More Functions of the Verb

Aptative/Abilitative

The *maka-* or *makapag-* affix indicates that the actor has the ability to do the action named by the verb base. *Ma-* is the goal-focus counterpart of both *maka-* and *makapag-* affixes. The following charts give examples of the *maka-* and *makapag-* sets.

Maka- Set

Focus	Verb	Actor	Object/Goal
actor	**Maka**bubuhat	siya	ng kotse.
	He can/is able to lift a car.		
goal	**Ma**bubuhat	niya	ang kotse.

The aspect forms of the maka-/ma- verbs are as follows, illustrated for the root basa 'to read.'

Aspect	Actor Focus	Object/Goal Focus
Infinitive	makabasa	mabasa
Completed	nakabasa	nabasa
Contemplated	makababasa	mababasa
	makakabasa	
Incompleted	nakababasa	nababasa
	nakakabasa	

Exercise

Supply the missing forms of the following verbs.

Aspect	Actor Focus	Object/Goal Focus
Root	kuha	basa
Infinitive		
Completed	nakakuha ,	
Contemplated		mababasa
Incompleted		

Makapag- Set

Focus	Verb	Actor	Object/Goal
Actor	**Makapag**dala kaya	kayo	ng pagkain.
	He was able to bring food.		
Goal	**Ma**dala	mo kaya	ang pagkain.

The aspect forms of makapag- and ma- -an verbs are as follows.

Aspect	Actor Focus	Object/Goal Focus
Root	*handa* 'to prepare'	
Infinitive	*makapaghanda*	*mahandaan*
Completed	*nakapaghanda*	*nahandaan*
Contemplated	*makapaghahanda*	*mahahandaan*
	makakapaghanda	
Incompleted	*nakapaghahanda*	*nahahandaan*
	nakakapaghanda	

Note that verbs having an *-an* goal focus affix (e.g. *laban*) get a *ma- ...-an* compound affix instead of just *ma-*. Note , too, that the *-ka-* of the affix *maka-* or *makapag-* may be reduplicated instead of the first syllable of the word base or root.

Maka- usually occurs with verb roots that take the *-um-* and *ma-* affixes, whereas *makapag-* usually occurs with verb roots that take the *mag-* affix.

Exercises

a. Supply the missing *maka-/makapag-*verbs. Note the type of aspect given for each verb.

1. **Nakakuha** (verb *kuha,*, completed) *si Patricio ng kawayan.*

2. _____ (verb *tulog,* incompleted) *ka ba kahit mainit?*

3. _____ (verb *tugtog,* contemplated) *si William ng gitara.*

4. _____ (verb *luto,* contemplated) *ba kayo ng morkon?*

5. _____ (verb *salita,* incompleted) *si Rosie ng Kastila.*

6. _____ (verb, *bili,* completed) *si Ruben ng Walkman.*

b. Change the following *maka-* sentences into *ma-* sentences.

1. *Nakakakain na siya ng gulay.* **Makakain na niya ang gulay.**

2. *Nakatatakbo na si Amy ng anim na milya.*

3. *Makakabili na siya ng bahay.*

4. *Nakakabasa na si Sam ng nobela sa Tagalog.*

5. *Nakakapagmaneho na siya ng trak.*

6. *Nakabubuhat na siya ng isang kabang bigas.*

c. Write five things you can do using *maka-/makapag-* sentences.

1.

2.

3.

4.

5.

d. Change your sentences into goal focus sentences if possible.

1.

2.

3.

4.

5.

Social-participative

Maki- is the actor-focus counterpart of the prefix *paki-* which makes the verb base a request form. Unlike *paki-*, however, *maki-* can also be used to ask permission to use or partake of something owned by someone. Where no one is addressed in a *paki-* request, the object may take a *ng* marker.

	Actor		**Object**
Pakiabot	mo	nga	ang asin.
Pakiabot		nga	ng asin.

Note the differences in the use of *maki-* in the following examples.

Request   **Maki**bili nga ako ng kartolina sa tindahan.
             Makikuha nga ako ng tubig.

Permission **Maki**tawag nga sa telepono ninyo.
             Makibasa nga ng diyaryo ninyo.
             Makiinom nga.

The various aspects may also be expressed with the *maki-* and *paki-* affixes. The following chart illustrates the occurrence of the different aspect forms with both affixes.

Aspect	*Maki-* + Verb Base	*Paki-* + Verb Base
Infinitive	*makibili*	*pakibili*
Completed	*nakibili*	*pinakibili*
Contemplated	*makikibili*	*pakikibili*
Incompleted	*nakikibili*	*pinakikibili*

In both the *maki-* and *paki-* forms, the last syllable of the affix instead of the first (consonant-)vowel of the base is reduplicated for the contemplated and incompleted aspects.

Exercises

a.   Give the correct form of the following *maki-* and *paki-* verbs as cued.

1.   *makikuha* (contemplated)

2.   *makilagay* (completed)

3.   *makikain* (contemplated)

4.   *makitulog* (incompleted)

5.   *makiligo* (incompleted)

6.   *pakiabot* (completed)

7.   *pakikuha* (contemplated)

8.   *pakidala* (incompleted)

9.   *pakiplantsa* (contemplated)

10. *pakidilig* (incompleted)

b.   You are temporarily staying at a friend's place. From the phrases below, construct *maki-* sentences that you may use.

Example: *tawag sa telepono   Makitawag nga sa telepono.*

1.   *gamit ng banyo*

2.   *maneho ng kotse*

3.   *bili ng pagkain*

4. *sampay ng damit*

5. *sakay sa kotse*

6. *basa ng diyaryo*

7. *gamit ng makinilya*

8. *gamit ng plantsa*

9. *lagay ng pagkain sa repridyerator*

10. *luto sa kalan*

c. Using *paki-* sentences, write some things that you may ask your friend or relative to do.

Example: *Pakisagot mo nga ang telepono.*

1.

2.

3.

4.

5.

The Addition of Enclitics

Order of Enciitics

Enclitics (e.g., *na, pa, nga,* etc.) normally occur after the first full word of the sentence. In a sentence with more than one enclitic, the normal order is as follows:

1	2	3	4		5	6	7		8
na	nga	din	lamang		daw	kaya	naman		sana
pa									pala
									yata

Functions of Enclitics

The usual meanings or uses of the enclitics are as follows:

1. *nga*   affirmation marker
2. *kaya*   speculation marker
3. *daw, raw*   reported speech marker
4. *din, rin*   'too'
5. *lang, lamang*   'only'
6. *na*   'already'
7. *pa*   'still'
8. *pala*   surprise marker
9. *sana*   optative marker
10. *yata*   uncertainty marker
11. *naman*   'instead'

Nga' *Nga'* when added to the sentence indicates affirmation, assertion, or emphasis.

*Pupunta **nga** siya sa party.*	(You're right,) he is going to the party.
*Guwapo **nga** siya.*	He certainly is handsome.
*Tama **nga** ang nanay.*	Mother is definitely right.
*Ikaw **nga** ang nasa parada.*	You (for sure) were the one in the parade.
*Kumanta **nga** ang artista.*	The actress did sing.

Exercise

Translate the following.

1. Ed really is a kind man.

2. He certainly is rich.

3. I do like warm weather.

4. He did write a novel.

5. Their house is really far away.

Daw *Daw/raw* marks indirect discourses. It means 'according to; it is said.' *Daw* indicates that the sentence represents what someone other than the speaker said. *Raw*, a variant form of *daw*, occurs after vowels.

*Maganda **raw** si Aleli.* It is said that Aleli is beautiful.
*Matigas **daw** ang ulo ni Nestor.* Someone said Nestor is hard-headed.

Exercise

Change the following sentences into statements that someone else had said.

1. *Pangit ang sine.*
2. *Umuulan.*
3. *Tumakbo siya sa maraton.*
4. *Nabasag ang pinggan.*
5. *Nahuli ang kriminal.*

Realization: *pala*   The use of *pala* in a sentence expresses a sudden realization or surprise at an unexpected event or happening. It follows one-syllable pronouns or other enclitics.

*Dumating **pala** si Romulo.*	So Romulo arrived.
*Kumain na **pala** ang Nanay.*	So Nanay already ate.
*O, heto na **pala** si Joe.*	Oh, here comes Joe.
*Aba, tapos ka na **pala**.*	Oh, so you're done.
*Oo nga **pala**, ano.*	Yeah, that's right.

Pala is also used to signal change of topic in a conversation.

Siyanga pala, umalis na siya.	And by the way, he left.
Oo nga pala, ako na.	Oh, yes, it's my turn.

Exercises

a. Translate the following into *pala* sentences.

Oh, yes, you're right, ...
1. the bus came late.
2. he won.

3. the letter arrived yesterday.

4. we won't have classes today.

5. I got the job.

b. Translate the following sentences using *pala* to introduce a new topic.

By the way, ...
1. did you get your promotion?

2. the new bank was robbed.

3. the policemen caught the burglar.

4. did you hear what happened to Joshua?

5. he wrote, finally.

Rejoinder: *din /rin* *Din* is commonly used to express similarity between two situations. It is usually translatable by 'too' or 'also'. A variant form is *rin*, which occurs after vowel sounds.

Maganda si Cora.	*Si Estelita **rin**.*
	*Maganda **rin** si Estelita.*
Cora is pretty.	And so is Estelita.
	Estelita is pretty, too.

Exercise

Supply the rejoinders to the following as cued.

1. *Matapang si Ben.*   (*si Jim*)

2. *Maalalahanin ang tatay niya.* (*ang nanay niya*)

3. *Masipag ang drayber nila.*   (*siya*)

4. *Matalino siya.*   (*ang mga anak niya*)

5. *Malakas ang ulan sa Oahu.*   (*sa Maui*)

Na and Pa as Time Markers   In general, *na* denotes completed action or action about to be performed while *pa* denotes non-completed, continuous, resumptive action, or action in addition to other actions, or action to be performed sometime in the future. *Pa* and *na* usually follow the first word in the predicate.

With non-verbal sentences beginning with time expressions, *na* denotes shortness of time, *pa* denotes length of time.

> *Bukas **pa** ang iksamin.*
> The exam is still tomorrow (there's plenty of time till then).

> *Bukas **na** ang iksamin.*
> The exam is already tomorrow (there's little time before then).

In imperative or command sentences, *na* denotes immediate performance of an action, *pa* denotes resumption or continuation of the action.

> *Kumain ka **na**.*   Eat now.
> *Kumain ka **pa**.*   Eat some more.

With verbs in the contemplated aspect, *na* and *pa* have the same meanings as in the previous paragraph. However, *pa* can have a second meaning, that the action expressed by the verb is an additional one not yet begun, to a series of other actions.

> *Kakain **na** ako.*   I'll eat now (I haven't eaten yet).
> *Kakain **pa** ako.*   I'll eat some more, or I'm still going to eat (because I've been doing other things and I haven't eaten yet).

With verbs in the incompleted aspect, *na* is equivalent to English 'already' and *pa* to 'still, yet.'

> *Kumakain **na** ako.*   I'm already eating.
> *Kumakain **pa** ako.*   I'm still eating.

With verbs in the completed aspect, *na* denotes completion of an action, sometimes unexpectedly prior to another action, while *pa* denotes an action performed in addition to a past action.

> *Kumain **na** ako.*   I have already eaten.
> *Kumain **pa** ako.*   I ate some more.

With adjectives, *na* indicates a non-existent quality before, whereas *pa* indicates a continuing quality.

*Maganda **na** siya.*	She's pretty now (she wasn't before).
*Maganda **pa** siya.*	She's still pretty.

With existentials (*may, mayroon, wala*), *na* indicates the existence of something which was non-existent before, whereas *pa* indicates the continuing existence of something. *Na* with *wala* means non-existence of something which existed before. *Pa* with *wala* means non-existence yet.

*May pera **na** siya.*	He now has money (he didn't before).
*Wala **na** siyang pera.*	He has no more money.
*May pera **pa** siya.*	He still has money.
*Wala **pa** siyang pera.*	He doesn't have money yet.

Exercise

Translate into English.

1. *Mamaya pa ang misa.*
2. *Malaki na ang bahay niya.*
3. *Malakas pa ang lolo niya.*
4. *Lumalakad na ang anak niya.*
5. *Masakit pa ang ulo niya.*
6. *Umalis na siya.*
7. *Maghain ka na.*
8. *Sa isang linggo pa ang piknik*
9. *Wala pa siyang asawa.*
10. *May utang pa ako.*
11. *Kakanta pa si Perlita.*
12. *Tatalog na siya sa tulay.*
13. *Mayroon na siyang puhunan.*
14. *Wala na siyang magulang.*
15. *Umuulan pa.*

Lang The degree marker *lang* and its variant *lamang* mean 'just, only.' When modifying a noun or adjective, *lang* has a belittling connotation, a depreciation of someone or someone's accomplishments. The variant *lamang* is seldom used in casual speech.

> *Guwapo si Dirk, pandak **lang**.*
> Dirk's good-looking, except he's short.

> *Sundalo **lang** siya.*
> He's only a soldier.

Exercise

Would you insert *lang* in the following sentences?

1. *Mahirap siya.*
2. *Doktor siya.*
3. *Mabait siya.*
4. *Mayabang siya.*
5. *Abogado siya.*
6. *Karpentero siya.*
7. *Tamad siya.*
8. *Kuripot siya.*
9. *Kargador siya.*
10. *Duwag siya.*

Naman *Naman* is used to express a contrast between two situations, a shift in role or viewpoint, a mild reproach (in imperative sentences), or a critical attitude. It is often glossed as 'on the other hand' or 'instead.'

(Contrast)	*Kuripot **naman** si Carmen.*
	Carmen (on the other hand) is stingy.
(Shift)	*Kumusta ka **naman**?*
	And how are you?
(Reproach)	*Tumahimik **naman** kayo.*
	Do keep quiet.

(Critical)   *Ang ingay **naman** dito!*
              How noisy it is here.

Exercise

Translate the following sentences using *naman.*

1. It's my turn.
2. He (on the other hand) is my cousin.
3. Please don't leave right away.
4. How lazy you are (and I don't like it).
5. I (on the other hand) don't have money.

Uncertainty: *yata'* *Yata* is used in statements to express uncertainty or lack of conviction.

Wala yatang tao.   There seems to be no one (I'm not sure).
Nagiginaw yata ang bata. The child seems cold (I'm not certain).

Exercise

Change the following statements into uncertain ones and translate into English.

1. *Mahal iyon.*   a.
                              b.
2. *Hindi siya darating.*   a.
                              b.
3. *Makipot ang damit.*   a.
                              b.
4. *Siksikan sa loob ng sine.* a.
                              b.
5. *Malaki ang utang niya.*   a.
                              b.

Sana   *Sana* is commonly used to express a hope.

*Umaraw **sana** bukas.*	I hope the sun shines tomorrow.
*Gumaling **sana** siya.*	I hope he gets well.
*Matulungin **sana** siya.*	I hope he's helpful.

Exercise

Change the following factual sentences into sentences expressing hope and translate into English.

1. *Umulan.*   a.

                           b.

2. *Masaya ang buhay niya.*   a.

                           b.

3. *Umalis siya.*   a.

                           b.

4. *Malaki na ang suweldo ko.*   a.

                           b.

5. *Madali ang iksamen.*   a.

                           b.

Speculation: *kaya'*   *Kaya* expresses speculation usually in questions.

*Darating **kaya** siya?*	Do you suppose he's coming?
*Manalo **kaya** siya?*	I wonder if he'll win.

Exercises

a.   Change the following statements into speculations and to English.

1. *Nahulog siya.*   a.

                           b.

2. *Nalunod ang aso.*   a.

                                b.

3. *Ninakaw ang pera.*   a.

                                b.

4. *Kumakain siya ng balut.*   a.

                                b.

5. *Nagsasabong siya.*   a.

                                b.

b. Insert the following enclitics in the sample sentence and translate the resulting sentence into English.

Example: *Bumili siya ng bahay.*

   (*daw*)   a. **Bumili daw siya ng bahay.**
            b. Someone said that he bought a house.

1. *na*   a.
       b.
2. *nga*   a.
       b.
3. *rin*   a.
       b.
4. *pala* a.
       b.
5. *kaya* a.
       b.
6. *pa*   a.
       b.
7. *lang* a.
       b.

8. *naman* a.

   b.

9. *yata* a.

   b.

10. *sana* a.

    b.

c. Translate the following into English expressing the closest correspondence to the meaning of the enclitics.

1. *Sa Linggo pa ang piyesta.*

2. *Sa Linggo na ang piyesta.*

3. *Iinitin ko na ang pagkain.*

4. *Iinitin ko pa ang pagkain.*

5. *Nasa bahay na si Rosa.*

6. *Nasa bahay pa si Rosa.*

7. *Kaalis pa lang ni David.*

8. *Saan ka pa pupunta?*

9. *Ang pulis man ay natakot din.*

10. *Kumain na nga siya.*

11. *Saan daw siya pupunta?*

12. *Ang mahal naman nito!*

13. *Tanghali na kasi siya nagising.*

14. *Tuloy nahuli siya sa klase.*

15. *Maganda pala ito, a.*

16. *Nagugutom yata ang bata.*

17. *Manalo sana si George.*

18. *Sila lang ba ang sasayaw?*

19. *Sila ba muna ang sasayaw?*

20. *Bukas din ng gabi, sasayaw sila.*

chapter 6

Complex Sentences: Conjoining

Complex sentences are combinations of two or more simple ones. We will look at two ways of combining sentences: *conjoining* the two sentences one after the other, and *embedding* one sentence inside another. In this chapter and the next, we look at conjoining; we discuss embedding in Chapter 8.

Conjoining

Conjoining can be as simple as joining the sentences using a *conjunctor* with hardly any change at all in the combined sentences.

Simple Sentences:	*Hinawakan ni Ben ang lapis. Sumulat siya.*
Conjunction:	*Hinawakan ni Ben ang lapis* **at** *sumulat siya.*
	Ben held the pencil, **and** he wrote.

The simple sentences are joined by the conjunctor *at*. The two sentences retain their equal standing syntactically with respect to one another, that is to say, neither is subsumed under the other. Here are more examples:

Humangin nang malakas **at** *bumagsak ang ulan.*
Nabuwal ang bote **at** *sumabog ang masamang amoy.*
Madilim ang langit, **kaya** *mainit ang ulo ni Damian.*
Nagsuka si Derek, **kasi** *nakaamoy siya ng bagoong.*

Exercises

a. Which sentences are examples of conjoining?

1. *Nalito si Mike at nasiraan naman ng loob si Don.*
2. *Inulan ang Maynila, at nilindol pa.*
3. *Maganda ang babaeng nakaupo sa pasigan.*
4. *Mapurol ang gulok na binili ni Max.*
5. *Sumama ang sikmura ni Joe, pero magaling na siya.*
6. *Tinanong si Dexter kung ayos na siya.*
7. *Inubos ni Jodi ang cake, kaya umatungal si Nini.*
8. *Ayaw ni Guy na uminom ng Canadian wine.*
9. *Kailangang magluto tayo ng patatas para sa bisiting puti.*
10. *Nalutas na rin ang pag-iyak-iyak ni Amanda.*

b. Complete these sentences by supplying the other basic sentence.

1. *Pinatay ni Joana ang ilaw, kaya*
2.   *kaya napaiyak si Perla.*
3. *Nagtatampo si Renato, dahil*
4.   *dahil malakas ang ulan.*
5. *Tumangos ang ilong niya, kasi*

The Function of Conjoining

Why conjoin sentences? What purpose does it serve?

Sentence conjoining allows for a more explicit expression of certain relationships between the events contained in the clauses. These relationships are expressed mainly through the conjunctors, and sometimes with the help of certain particles. A familiar relationship is *effect*. Here's an example:

Effect   *Napatid ang lubid,* **kaya' nahulog si Angela.**
                     The rope snapped, so Angela fell down.

The conjunctor *kaya'* makes explicit the fact that the second event is a direct result of the event expressed in the first conjunct.

The rest of this chapter is about the range of relationships between conjoined clauses in Tagalog. But first, let us look at how some of them are expressed in English. In the examples below, give short names for these relationships. The first is done for you.

1. The man looked suspicious, so Roberta followed him. (effect)
2. Life takes on a nasty twist, when liquor stores close early.
3. Jonathan took the bus while Joseph hitched a ride.
4. Ben lost his job, and what's more, he couldn't find his car keys.
5. Yvan is not a big man, but he's a fine athlete.
6. Yvan is a fine athlete, although he's not a big man.
7. Write, or call collect.
8. I'll cook sinigang for you, if you trim my gumamelas.
9. Because you trimmed my gumamelas, I'll cook sinigang for you.
10. He's not been the same since his pet Tiger disappeared.

The Conjunctors

In conjoining, the relationship between the clauses is expressed by the conjunctor.

Clause	**Conjunctor**	**Clause**
Bumuhos ang ulan	**kaya** (Effect)	*nabasa si Jane.*
Mag-jogging ka	**para** (Purpose)	*lumakas ang katawan mo.*

Enclitic particles may occur in these constructions. Some of these particles are optional. Both *kasi* and *tuloy* in the example below are optional.

Kain **kasi** *nang kain si Walter, kaya* **tuloy** *nananaba siya.*

In some cases, the enclitic makes the sentence sound better.

Awkward: *Matanda na si Doug, pero mahilig siyang magdisko.*
Better: *Matanda na si Doug, pero mahilig* **pa** *siyang magdisko.*

In other cases, the enclitics are required to complete the expression of a particular relationship. In the second example below, *naman* puts the second clause in contrast with the first clause.

> Neutral: *Nagsigarilyo si Pepe, at nagtabako si Daniel.*
> Contrast: *Nagsigarilyo si Pepe, at nagtabako **naman** si Daniel.*

Our focus is the clause that carries the conjunctor; this is typically the second clause. We start with the neutral case of no semantic relationship or dependency between the clauses.

Neutral

> Conjunctor: *at*   'and'
>
> Example: *Namili ako kahapon **at** nagpunta ako sa beach.*

The most common use of *at* as conjunctor is to express a neutral relationship between the clauses. It merely expresses the observation that another event occurred simultaneously in time or in close proximity.

> *Nalagas ang mga dahon **at** nalaglag ang mga bunga.*
> *Kumuha si Manuel ng diyaryo **at** hinampas niya ang langaw.*

Exercises

a. Translate the following sentences.

1. Richard put his feet up, and Steve grabbed a bottle of beer.
2. Simon opened the wine, and Martha prepared the glasses.
3. The car halted to a stop, and the engine conked out.
4. Wayne looked at the flat tire, and he kicked it.
5. Marsha stared at the empty wine bottle and she smiled.

b. Supply neutral second clauses.

1. *Tumakas si Ben at*
2. *Nagkape si Ana at*

3. *Nanuod ng sine si Minda at*

4. *Kumuha ng kampit si Edgar at*

5. *Tumayo si Oscar at*

6. *Tumikhim si Josie at*

7. *Binuksan ni Roberto ang pinto at*

8. *Namatay ang mga ilaw at*

Explanation

Conjunctor: *at* 'and'

Example: *Salamat sa Diyos **at** dumating si Digna.*

The conjunctor *at* is also used to introduce an explanatory clause. *At* here is roughly equivalent to English *that* in the sentence "Good that you have arrived." Here are more examples:

> *Mabuti na lang **at** umalis si Ben.*
> *Magaling naman **at** nakayari si Manuel.*
> *Malas na lang **at** umulan.*
> *Sayang **at** wala ka sa Sabado.*
> *Milagro **at** sumama sa atin si Fernando.*

The second clause can be any declarative sentence. But the predicate of the first clause appears to be limited to a small set of "judgment" adjectives, as in the above sentences, and verbs expressing emotions as in the following list (all in the incompleted aspect):

nagsisisi	regrets
natutuwa, nagagalak	glad
nagtataka	wonders
nasusuya, nabubuwisit, napipika, naasar	upset, furious
nahihiya	shy
nalulungkot	sad
nagagalit	angry
nanghihinayang	feeling sorry

114 Conjoining

Exercises

a. Supply appropriate explanation clauses to the following sentences.

1. *Nagsisisi si Alip at*
2. *Natutuwa si Mayor at*
3. *Nagagalak ako at*
4. *Nagtataka ang Tatay at*
5. *Napipika si Tom at*

b. Answer the following questions with explanation clauses.

1. *Bakit nasusuya si Rosie?*   **Nasusuya si Rosie at**
2. *Bakit nahihiya si Zelda?*
3. *Bakit nalulungkot na naman si Ester?*
4. *Bakit nagalit ang pulis?*
5. *Bakit nakangitisi Amy?*

c. Give five events you'd normally be thankful for.

Example: *Mabuti na lang at nanalo si Flo sa binggo.*

1. *Mabuti na lang at*
2. *Salamat na lang at*
3. *Nakakatuwa naman at*
4.
5.

d. Give five events you'd normally regret happening.

Example: *Sayang at nakawala ang isda.*

1. *Sayang at*
2. *Malas at*

3. *Nakakahinayang at*

4. *Nakakainis at*

5. *Nakakalungkot at*

Contrast

Conjunctors: *at...naman*   in contrast; meanwhile
                    samantalang...naman

Examples:
*Nagduktor si Miriam **at** nag-abogado **naman** si Dante.*
*Nakikain si Dwayne **samantalang** nakitulog **naman** si Paul.*

The second clause is in direct contrast to the first clause. *Samantalang...naman* expresses a stronger contrast than *at...naman.*

*Inubo si Curtis **at** na-flu **naman** si Alfonso.*
*Puti ang isinuot ni Nora **at** rosas **naman** ang isinuot ni Cora.*
*Nagmatigas si Igor, **samantalang** nagtapat **naman** si Natasha.*
*Nakatulog nang mahimbing si Daniel, **samantalang** dilat na dilat*
    ***naman** ang mga mata ni Nina.*
*Katahimik ni Jack **samantalang** kabida **naman** ng asawa niya.*

Exercises

a.   Provide contrasting clauses.

1. *Katalas ng ulo ni Jethro at **kapurol naman ng ulo ni Yuki.***

2. *Katayog ni Marco samantalang*

3. *Nagkabaon-baon sa utang si Jack at*

4. *Mahusay makipag-usap si Arthur samantalang*

5. *Kilalang abogado si Ken at*

6. *Mahusay magpiyano si Perla at*

7. *Masayang kausap si Dexter samantalang*

8. *Sumikat na mabuti si Nora samantalang*

b. Form sentences that put in contrast the members of the pairs.

1. *Gandhi - Mao*

2. *Los Angeles - New York*

3. *alak - beer*

4. *Star Wars - Star Trek*

5. *radyo - telebisyon*

6. *tenis - golp*

7. *tag-ulan - tag-araw*

8. *langit - lupa*

9. *araw - gabi*

10. *mayaman - mahirap*

Incremental

Conjunctor:	*(at)*	and what's more
Particles:	*na* (first clause)	
	pa (second clause)	
Example:	*Binaha **na** nga ang Maynila, **at** nilindol **pa**.*	

The second clause expresses the idea that the event "adds insult to injury," so to speak. The use of *na...at...pa* is roughly equivalent to the English "on top of it all, and what's more" as in "John lost his job, and what's more, his wife left him." The conjunctor *at* is optional, and in fact, is typically left out.

*Nalugi **na** nga si Damian, **at** iniwanan **pa** ng asawa.*
*Kinupkop mo **na** ang walanghiya, ninakawan ka **pa**.*
*Pinakain mo **na** sa palad mo, kinagat ka **pa**.*
*Ipinagtanggol **na** nga ni Joe si Max, nilabanan **pa** siya.*
*Tinulungan **na** nga kita, sinisi mo **pa** ako.*

Exercises

a. Give five depressing events, using the construction *na...(at)...pa*.

Example:
   Nalumpo na nga si Melvin, nasagasaan pa ang mga kamay niya.

1.

2.

3.

4.

5.

b. Now let's talk about one good fortune after another.

Examples:
   Maganda na nga ang napangasawa niya, mayaman pa.
   Mababait na nga ang mga anak ni Dario, marurunong pa.
   Nakatuklas na nga siya ng mina sa lupa niya, nanalo pa siya sa sweepstakes

1.

2.

3.

4.

5.

Supplemental

Conjunctors:	*at saka*	and also
	at gayon din	and likewise
	at...rin	and...too

Example: *Nagluto si Karla ng pansit, **at saka** gumawa siya ng puto.*

The second clause describes an event or states a condition that supplements the first clause.

*Naligo ako sa beach, **at saka** nagsiyaping ako sa Ala Moana.*
*Namili ako sa Mabini, **at** namili **rin** ako sa Makati.*
*Humusay si Esper sa History, **at gayon din,** humusay siya sa Math.*
*Nagmano si Rafael sa Tatay, **at saka** nagmano rin siya kay Kuya.*

At gayon din is formal; avoid it.

Exercises

a. Determine the type of relationship the second clause maintains with the first clause: neutral, explanation, contrast, incremental or supplemental.

1. *Salamat sa Diyos at huminto ang ulan!*
2. *Dumating ang Nanay at hinahanap ka.*
3. *Napakalaking babae ni Ana, samantalang kaliit naman ng asawa niya.*
4. *Nagalit si Padre Damaso at malabnaw daw ang tsokolate niya.*
5. *Mukhang donya kung umasta si Seta, pero wala naman sila.*
6. *Nagalit ang Nanay at hindi ka raw sumusulat.*
7. *Sinundo nila si Ben sa airport, at saka dinala siya sa hotel.*
8. *Trabaho nang trabaho si Franco, at gasta naman nang gasta si Debbie.*
9. *Maganda na nga ang panahon sa Hawaii, mababait pa ang mga tao.*
10. *Mura na, matibay pa.*

b. Supply the appropriate conjunctor and particle.

(Neutral) 1. *Tumakbo ka sa tindahan, (?) bumili ka ng Coke.*

(Explanation) 2. *Sayang (?) natalo si Eddie.*

(Contrast) 3. *Napakasuwabe ni Cora (?) napakagarapal (?) ni Jim.*

(Incremental) 4. *Nagagalit (?) nga si Manny, sinulsulan mo (?).*

(Supplemental) 5. *Nagdasal ako sa Diyos, (?) ko siya kinausap.*

(Neutral) 6. *Dinampot ni Melba ang mga bulaklak, (?) inihagis niya sa mga tao.*

(Contrast) 7. *Naglaro ng tenis si Jonathan, (?) nag-golp (?) si Dan.*

(Supplemental) 8. *Nag-swimming si Dick, (?) nag-swimming (?) si Mark.*

(Incremental) 9. *Madulas (?) nga ang daan, madilim (?).*

(Explanation) 10. *Mainam naman (?) malakas ka na.*

Effect

Conjunctors:	*kaya (tuloy)*	so therefore; so now
	kaya (nga ba)	
	kaya (ngayon)	

Particle: *kasi* (first clause)

Example: *Matiyaga (kasi) si Dindo, kaya (tuloy) yumaman siya.*

The second clause expresses the effect of the first clause. *Kasi* is optional, but if it occurs, it must follow the first constituent of the first clause. The particles *tuloy*, *nga ba*, and *ngayon* optionally occur after the conjunctor *kaya*.

Exercises

a. A sentence in A may be the cause of any number of effects in B. Match them.

A	B
1. *Umulan nang malakas*	a. *kaya tuloy minalat siya.*
2. *Nahulog siya sa kama*	b. *kaya binaha ang Maynila.*
3. *Kumain kasi siya ng seafood*	c. *kaya inaantok siya.*
4. *Natapilok si Minda*	d. *kaya nasunog ang sinaing.*
5. *Nanalo si Ester sa binggo*	e. *kaya masakit ang likod niya.*
6. *Napuyat siya*	f. *kaya nangati siya.*
7. *Nakapunta si Rey saTokyo*	g. *kaya masayang-masaya siya.*
8. *Nakapasa si Zenon sa exam*	h. *kaya yumabang siya.*
9. *Kumanta si Ana*	i. *kaya napilay siya.*
10. *Nagkasakit ang Tatay niya*	j. *kaya umuwi siya.*

b. Answer the following questions with effect clauses.

Example:
   Question: *Nang mabusan ng tubig si Wilf, ano'ng nangyari?*
   Answer: *Nang mabusan ng tubig si Wilf, natauhan siya.*

1. *Nang mahulog siya sa kama, ano ang nangyari?*
2. *E nang umulan nang pagkalakas-lakas, ano'ng nangyari?*
3. *Nang kumain siya ng balot, ano'ng nangyari sa kaniya?*
4. *E nang marinig niya ang balita, ano ang nangyari?*
5. *At nang bumangga sila sa poste, ano'ng nangyari sa kotse?*
6. *E nang pinatay niya ang mga ilaw, ano'ng nangyari?*
7. *Nang lumindol sa Maynila, ano ang nangyari?*
8. *Nang mahulog si George sa swimming pool, ano'ng nangyari sa kaniya?*
9. *Nang tamaan siya ng baseball sa ulo, ano'ng naging resulta?*
10. *Nang magkita sila sa plaza, ano'ng kinalabasan?*

Cause

Conjunctor: *kasi*   because
                 dahil kasi, dahil sa
                 kung dangan kasi
                 papaano kasi
                 sapagka't
                 palibhasa'y

Example: *Napangiti si Ramon, **kasi** naalala niya si Nancy.*

The cause clause attributes a cause or offers a reason or explanation for the event in the first sentence.

*Nahuli ako, **kasi** naplatan kami.*
*Hindi nakatapos si Mario, **kasi** nagbulakbol siya.*
*Nanlaki ang mga mata ni Nancy, **kasi** hindi siya makapaniwala.*
*Hindi aasenso si Perla, **kasi** masyado siyang mahiyain.*

The conjunctors *sapagka't* and *palibhasa'y* are rarely used in casual conversation.

In a cause conjunction, the first clause is an effect clause, and the second is cause. Conversely in an effect conjunction (discussed earlier), the first clause is cause and the second is effect.

Cause Conjunction
Nahuli ako (effect), *kasi* (cause conjunctor) *naplatan kami* (cause).

Effect Conjunction
Naplatan kami (cause), *kaya* (effect conjunctor) *nahuli ako* (effect).

Exercises

a. Make convincing excuses for the following events. Use cause conjunctors.

1. *Nasunog ang sinaing*
2. *Pinalitan ka na namin*
3. *Hindi ka na kasama sa lakad*
4. *Hindi dumating si Dante*
5. *Hindi ko nayari ang trabaho*
6. *Hindi kita natawagan*
7. *Gusto kong isauli ito*
8. *Nahuli* (late) *ako*
9. *Isinauli ko ang napulot kong pera*
10. *Naiwala ko ang libro*

b. Answer effect clauses to the following cause clauses.

Example:
    Q: *Matiyaga si Lilia, kaya ...*
    A: *Matiyaga si Lia,* **kaya natuto siya agad.**

1. *Maghapong kumanta si Perla, kaya ...*
2. *Tumama sa stock market si Daniel, kaya ...*

3. *Dumami ang problema ni Imelda, kaya ...*

4. *Tumanggap ng malaking tip ang wayter, kaya ...*

5. *Nagkagulo ang mga tao sa parada, kaya ...*

6. *Naibangga na naman ni Amelia ang kotse, kaya ...*

7. *Parami nang parami ang mga tao, kaya ...*

8. *Pinag-usapan nila ng mabuti si Martin, kaya ...*

9. *Nakatanggap ng mabuting balita si Jasmine, kaya ...*

10. *Binawasan ang suweldo ng mga drayber, kaya ...*

Counter-Expectation

Type A Counter-expectation

Conjunctors:	*pero*	but
	nguni't	
	subali't	
	datapwa't	
	gayon (pa) man	

Particles: *na* (first clause)
             pa (second clause)

Example: *Mayaman **na** siya, **pero** nagtatrabaho **pa** rin siya.*

The first clause is a statement that carries certain expectations. The second clause is *not* one of these expectations. It asserts the opposite of one of the expectations. In the first example, the expectation is that anyone who has become rich should stop working.

Sentences in context give rise to any number of expectations. A simple sentence like the following may have any number of expectations.

	Possible Expectations
Nakatayo na si Arthur.	*Handa na siyang lumakad.*
	Gusto na niyang umuwi.
	Maaabot na niya ang ilaw.
	Mas malaki siya kay Ramon.

These expectations may turn out to be false. That is, their negation may be true, giving rise to counter-expectations.

Nakatayo **na** si Arthur, **pero** hindi **pa** siya handang lumakad.
Nakatayo **na** si Arthur, **pero** ayaw **pa** niyang umuwi.
Nakatayo **na** si Arthur, **pero** hindi **pa** niya maaabot ang ilaw.
Nakatayo **na** si Arthur, **pero** maliit **pa** rin siya kay Charo.

These sentences are much better with the particles *na* in the first clause, and the particle *pa* in the second clause. Another set of particles that occurs in counter-expectations is *nga* in the first clause and *naman* in the second clause.

Luma **nga** ang bahay, pero maganda **naman**.
Magsasaka **nga** si Daniel, pero pino **naman**.
Masaya **nga** sa Maynila, pero mainit **naman**.

Exercise

A. Give reasonable expectations for each of the following sentences.

Example:
    Nag-asawa na si Ben. a. *Responsable na siya.*
                            b. *Hindi na siya mapag-alis ng bahay.*

1. *Nakayari na (ng pag-aaral) si Tirso.*

   a.

   b.

2. *Nakabihis na si Marcia.*

   a.

   b.

3. *Nakalabas na sa ospital si Rafael.*

   a.

   b.

4. *Tapos na ang programa.*

   a.

   b.

5. *Umaga na.*

   a.

   b.

B. Form conjunctions with counter-expectations using the sentences and expectations you supplied in Exercise A.

Example (based on the example in Exercise A):
   a. *Nag-asawa na si Ben, pero hindi pa rin siya responsable.*
   b. *Nag-asawa na si Ben, pero mapag-alis pa rin siya ng bahay.*

1. a.

   b.

2. a.

   b.

3. a.

   b.

4. a.

   b.

5. a.

   b.

The conjunctors *nguni't, datapwa't,* and *subali't* are too formal for use in everyday speech.

Type B Counter-expectation

Conjunctor:	*at*	and
Particle:	*pa* (second clause)	

   Example: *Dumating si Oscar kahapon,* **at** *nakakotse* **pa!**

As in Type A counter-expectation, the cause clause in Type B constructions contain a statement that is not expected to occur with the first clause.

Nagtatakbo si Mario, **at** *lumingon* **pa!**
Kumanta si Ana sa entablado, **at** *sumayaw* **pa!**
Tumayo si Satur sa pintuan, **at** *namaywang* **pa!**
Binigyan na si Ben ng pabor, **at** *nag-complain* **pa!**

In speech, the particle *pa* in the second clause is heavily stressed. The expectations are:

Dapat e hindi na lumingon pa si Mario.
Dapat e hindi na sumayaw pa si Ana.
Dapat e hindi na namaywang pa si Satur.
Dapat e hindi na nag-complain pa si Ben.

They are the negatives of the second clauses.

A common use of the second clause of an *at...pa* conjunction is to express
sarcasm. The examples below express the idea that the speaker does not
believe that the person spoken about is capable of performing the action, or
that he considers it wrong or inappropriate for him to do so.

Aba, at nakakotse pa!
Aba, at naka-Amerikana pa!
At nag-ambisyon pa!
At gusto pang manloko!
Tumawa pa!

Type C Counter-expectation

Conjunctor:	*imbis na*	instead of
	sa halip na	

Example:	*Nanuod ng TV si Glenda, **sa halip na** magluto.*

The second clause states the expectation, but the conjunctor eliminates it
as an occurrence; what actually happened is stated in the first clause.

*Nagwaldas ng salapi si Dante, **sa halip na** nag-aral na mabuti.*
*Natulog si Minda, **imbis na** nagbantay siya.*
*Nag-panic ang tour guide, **sa halip na** nag-kalma.*
*Namutla si Paquito, **sa halip na** namula.*

The expectations are:

Dapat na nag-aral na mabuti si Dante.
Dapat na nagbantay si Minda.
Dapat na nag-kalma ang tour guide.
Dapat e namula si Paquito.

In this type of counter-expectation, the second clause states the expectation
which the conjunctor negates. In the previous two types discussed, the
second clause states the opposite of the expectation.

Exercises

a. State the expectations.

1. *Nakabukas na ang mga bintana, pero kainit pa rin sa kuwarto.*

2. *Disyembre na, pero maulan pa rin.*

3. *Hindi nakapag-aral si Amado, gayunman, karunong niya.*

4. *Umirap na si Jane, at umingos pa!*

5. *Sinipa na ni Marco ang pusa, tinadyakan pa!*

6. *Uminom pa uli siya ng alak, sa halip na mag-almusal.*

7. *Nagmatigas si Deo, imbis na humingi ng tawad.*

8. *Nagtuloy pa kasi siya sa kabilang pampang, sa halip na bumalik.*

9. *Hey, bagong-taon na naman, pero wala pang nobya si Rico.*

10. *Anim na oras nang naglalaro si Jeffrey, pero hindi pa siya pagod.*

b. Based on the expectation in the similarly numbered sentences above, answer the following with *oo* or *hindi/wala.*.

1. *Mainit ba sa kuwarto?*

2. *Dapat bang maulan kung Disyembre? (sa Pilipinas)*

3. *Karunong ba ni Amado?*

4. *Umingos ba si Jane?*

5. *Dapat bang tadyakan pa ang pusang sinipa na?*

6. *Nag-almusal ba siya?*

7. *Humingi ba ng tawad si Deo?*

8. *Hindi ba bumalik si Minda?*

9. *May nobya ba si Rico noong nakaraang taon?*

10. *Kung anim na oras nang naglalaro ang isang tao, dapat bang pagod na siya?*

c. Write some sarcastic remarks. You may need one someday.

1. *At gusto pang matutong magsalita ng Ingles!*

2. *At nagsimba pa kunwari!*

3.

4.

5.

6.

Counter-Assumption

Conjunctor:	*kahit (na)*	although; in spite of the fact that
	gayong	
	samantala	
	bagama't	

Particles:	*(pa)(rin) ... (na)*
	(na) ... (pa)(rin)

Example:	*Mabigat si Alejandro,* **kahit** *payat siya.*

The first clause is a statement with some assumptions, and the second clause states the opposite of one of the assumptions. In the example above, the assertion in the first clause that Alejandro is heavy carries the assumption (at least in the mind of the speaker) that he could not have a slim physique. The second clause states that he in fact is slim.

Study the following conjunctions:

Mahilig **pa rin** *si Doug sa laro,* **kahit na** *matanda* **na** *siya.*
    Assertion: *Mahilig si Doug sa laro.*
    Assumption: *Bata pa siya.*
    Counter-Assumption: *Matanda na siya.*

Maganda **pa** *si Digna,* **gayong** *pito* **na** *ang anak niya.*
    Assertion: *Maganda si Digna.*
    Assumption: *Kakaunti ang anak niya.*
    Counter-Assumption: *Marami na siyang anak.*

Madilim **na,** **samantalang** *maaga* **pa.**
    Assertion: *Madilim na.*
    Assumption: *Gabi na.*
    Counter-Assumption: *Maaga pa.*

Exercise

Extract the assumption from the clause that contains the conjunctor.

1. *Nag-swimming si Amado, kahit may sakit siya.*
2. *Gayong natalo siya, nakangiti pa rin si Marcial.*
3. *Kahit nanalo siya, masama pa rin ang loob ni Bob.*
4. *Nag-aalala pa rin si Minda, samantalang malakas na ang Tatay.*
5. *Malakas ang katawan ni Martha, kahit payat siya.*
6. *Nakakulong pa rin si Dencio, gayong maimpluwensiya ang Tatay niya.*
7. *Kahit bata pa siya, mature na ang pag-iisip ni Rita.*
8. *Napakagaling na sa Algebra ni Elenita, gayong Grade 3 pa lang siya.*
9. *Umuwi na sa Hawaii si Patricia, gayong nakakailang araw pa lang siya sa New Jersey.*
10. *Lasing na si Chris, gayong isang serbesa pa lang ang naiinom niya.*

The counter-expectation clause is the assertion in a counter-assumption conjunction. The counter-assumption clause is the assertion in a counter-expectation conjunction. This is illustrated in the following sentences.

Counter-assumption: *Nagtatrabaho pa rin siya, kahit mayaman na.*
Counter-expectation: *Mayaman na siya, pero nagtatrabaho pa rin siya.*

Exercises

a. Replace the second clauses in the previous exercise with counter-expectations.

1. *Nag-swimming si Amado,* **pero takot siya sa tubig.**
2.
3.
4.

5.

6.

7.

8.

9.

10.

b. The sentences below are either counter-expectations or counter-assumptions. Change one form into the other.

1. *Masarap maglangoy, kahit na medyo maginaw.*

2. *Hatinggabi na, pero marami pa ring tao.*

3. *Sasama ako sa inyo, kahit na alam kong wala tayong pag-asa.*

4. *Tumilaok na ang mga manok, kahit hindi pa umaga.*

5. *Nagmamaneho na siya, pero wala pa siyang lisensiya.*

6. *Inani na ang mga repolyo, kahit maliliit pa.*

7. *Tuyo na ang mga sibuyas, pero wala pa ang mga mamimili.*

8. *Maputi na ang buhok ni Gloria kahit na hindi pa siya katandaan.*

c. Below are counter-expectation or counter-assumption clauses. Give as many appropriate assertions (first clauses) as you can for each of them. Consult an informant about common assumptions and expectations under the given circumstances. Expectations and assumptions are difficult to learn, but they are useful to know.

1. *...kahit matanda na siya.*

2. *...pero matanda na siya.*

3. *...kahit bata pa lang siya.*

4. *...pero bata pa lang siya.*

5. *...kahit lalaki siya.*

6. *...kahit babae siya.*

7. *...kahit dayuhan siya.*

8. ...*pero dayuhan siya.*

9. ...*kahit may asawa na siya.*

10. ...*pero may asawa na siya.*

Purpose

Conjunctor:	*para (noon / sa gayon (ay))*	so that
	upang (noon / sa gayon (ay))	
	at nang (noon / sa gayon (ay))	

Example: *Magpraktis kang mabuti, **para** humusay ka.*

The second clause serves as a purpose for carrying out the first clause. The linker *ay* may be contracted to *'y* or entirely omitted.

*Kumain ka ng marami, **para noon** hindi ka gutumin.*
*Nagpaplastik surgery si Carmen, **para** bumata siya.*
*Magtiyaga tayo, **at nang sa gayo'y** bumuti ang buhay natin.*
*Matuto tayong magsakripisyo, **para** umunlad ang Pilipinas.*

Upang and *sa gayon* are infrequent in informal speech.

Exercises

a. Answer the following questions with purpose clauses.

1. *Bakit kailangang kumain tayo ng maraming gulay?*

2. *Para ano't pupunta ka pa?*

3. *Bakit dapat tayong magtulung-tulong?*

4. *Para ano't nagjo-jogging ka?*

5. *Bakit pupunta ka sa Mindanao?*

6. *Para ano't babalik ka sa Pilipinas?*

7. *Para ano't nagpapakabuti tayo?*

8. *Para ano't tinutulungan mo siya?*

9. *Bakit ayaw mo siyang tulungan?*
10. *Para ano't inimbita mo pa si Gilbert?*

b. Answer the following questions.

1. *Ano'ng ginagawa ni Estelita para bumata siya?*
2. *Ano ba ang dapat gawin para maging kaibigan ko siya?*
3. *Ano ba ang gagawin ko para mayari ko ang trabaho ko?*
4. *Ano ba ang maaring gawin ni Ursula para malapit saTatay mo?*
5. *Ano ba ang unang gagawin para lumakas ako?*
6. *Ano ba ang dapat gawin para huminto ang pag-iyak ni Nina?*
7. *Ano raw ang kailangang gawin para manalo si Ben sa eleksiyon?*
8. *Ano kaya ang kailangang gawin para maging maligaya?*
9. *Ano kaya ang kailangang gawin para yumaman?*
10. *Ano raw ang kailangang gawin para makaakyat tayo sa langit?*

Alternation

| Conjunctor: | *o* | or |
| | *o kung hindi man* | or if not |

| Example: | *Sumulat ka, **o** tumawag ka ng long distance.* |

The second conjunct is offered as an alternative to the first. The particle *kaya* occurs optionally in one or the other clause.

*Pupunta ako sa inyo, **o kung hindi man** magpapasabi ako.*
*Si Fabian ang gawin nating presidente, **o** kaya si Angelo.*
*Maghimagas muna kayo, **o** uminom kaya kayo ng kape.*
*Magmadyong kaya tayo, **o** magbaraha na lang.*

Exercise

a. Offer alternatives to the following suggestions.

1. *Magsine kaya tayo, o*

2. *Magbakasyon ka kaya, o*

3. *Magtinda ka kaya sa palengke, o*

4. *Lumuwas ka sa Maynila, o*

5. *Nagsapalaran siguro si Damina sa Mindanao, o*

6. *Nabaril yata si Mitsiko, o*

7. *Iprito mo kaya ang isda, o*

8. *Nasa beach siguro si Egbert, o*

9. *Nakulong siguro si Marion ng ulan, o*

10. *Uminom ka kaya ng aspirin, o*

Conditional

Conjunctors:	*(ka)pag*	if; just in case
	kung	
	kung (saka-)sakali (man) at	
	sa sandaling	the moment
	oras na	
	basta't	as long as
	tuwing	every time

Example: *Kakandidato si Ben, **kung** hihilingin ng mga tao.*

The second clause expresses a condition that must be satisfied if the first clause is to be true.

*Pakakasal ako sa iyo, **pag** puti ng uwak.*
*Pupunta ako sa parke, **kung** hihinto ang ulan.*
*Pagsasabihan ko si Damian, **oras na** makita ko siya.*
*Umaasim ang sikmura ni Joana, **tuwing** makikita niya si Dan.*

(Saka-)sakali (at) adds to the remoteness of the plausibility of the condition.

> *Tatawagan kita,* **kung saka-sakali ma't** *madadaan uli ako rito.*
> *Babalatuhan kita,* **kung sakali't** *palarin ako.*

The conditional second clause, when introduced by *kung*, may be used alone to express a wish.

> *Kung president lang sana ako.*
> *Kung milyonaryo lang ako.*
> *Kung may kilala lang sana ako sa City Hall.*
> *Kung napangasawa sana kita.*

Used with the conjunctor *at*, the conditional expresses a dare or a challenge.

> *At kung hindi ako umalis (, ano'ng gagawin mo)?*
> *At kung kasalanan ni Julio (, ano ngayon)?*
> *At kung masamang babae si Marta (, ano'ng pakialam mo)?*
> *At kung ayoko?*

Exercises

a. Answer the following questions with conditional clauses.

1. *Kailan uuwi si Bob?*

   Uuwi si Bob kung tatawagan mo.

2. *Paano makakayari ng trabaho si Bob?*

3. *Paano matututo si Syl?*

4. *Kailan palalabasin si Carlo?*

5. *Paano lalaki ang mga halaman?*

6. *Paano uunlad ang Pilipinas?*

7. *Kailan lilinis ang Maynila?*

8. *Kailan igagalang ang mga pulitiko?*

9. *Paano mababago ang pagtingin sa Amerika?*

10. *Paano ako makatutulong sa kapwa?*

b. Answer the following questions as illustrated in Sentence 1.

1. *Ano ang mangyayari kung lilindol sa California?*

   Maraming masasaktan kung lilindol sa California.

2. *Ano ang gagawin mo oras na makita mo si Carla?*

3. *Ano ang nangyayari tuwing uulan sa Maynila?*

4. *Ano ang mangyayari sa sandaling makawala si Ponti?*

5. *Ano'ng gagawin mo kung saka-sakali't maging milyunaryo ka?*

6. *Ano ang gagawin mo oras na mamatay ang ilaw?*

7. *Ano ang gagawin ni Edgar oras na dumating siya sa New York?*

8. *Ano raw ang mangyayari kung sasabog ang rebolusyon bukas?*

9. *Ano ang dapat gawin kapag nakaamoy ka ng chlorine gas?*

10. *Ano ang nangyayari tuwing kabilugan ng buwan?*

Temporal

These constructions express a temporal relationship between the events of the component clauses. There are a number of possibilities: the event of the second clause may have started earlier or later or simultaneously with the event of the first clause. The conjunction may focus on the fact that both events are ongoing, or that they will terminate simultaneously.

Simultaneous start

Conjunctors:	*mula nang / mula pa noong*	since
	sapul nang / sapul pa noong	
	buhat nang / buhat pa noong	

Examples:

*Namayat na si Dindo, **buhat nang** iwanan siya ni Tarcila.*
*Naging tahimik si Narding, **buhat nang** masagasaan siya ng kalesa.*
*Umunti na ang mga bata dito, **sapul pa noong** magkaroon ng elektrisidad.*
*Bumabang lalo ang tingin ko sa kanya, **buhat nang** iwan niya si Virgilio.*

Simultaneous ongoing

Conjunctors: *habang*   while
                      samantala

Examples:

> *Magtiis mamaluktot **habang** maikli ang kumot.*
> *Kumakanta pa si Emma **habang** nagbabasa ng Aztec script.*
> *Pumipito si Roger **habang** naglalakad sa dilim.*
> *Tumatagaktak ang pawis ni Nestor **habang** nag-iisip.*
> *Nag-volunteer si Ali, **samantalang** wala siyang trabaho.*

Simultaneous termination

Conjunctor: *hanggang (sa)*   until
                = *habang hindi*   while not
Examples:

> *Dumito ka muna, **hanggang sa** makakita ka ng trabaho.*
> *Dumito ka muna, **habang hindi** ka nakakakita ng trabaho.*
> *Nagtrabaho si Jaime, **hanggang** lumawit ang dila niya.*

Sequential   The event in the second clause occurs after the event in the first clause.

Conjunctors: *bago (pa)*   even before
                nang   when
                at pagkatapos   and afterwards

Examples:

> *Sunog na ang bahay **nang** dumating ang mga bumbero.*
> *Nakatakbo na ang magnanakaw, **bago** dumating ang pulis.*
> *Nagsalita si Deo, **at pagkatapos**, tumutol si Martin.*
> *Nasa daan na si Max, **nang** bumuhos ang malakas na ulan.*

Reverse sequential   The event of the second clause occurs before the event of the first clause.

Conjunctor: *pagkatapos*   after

Examples:

> *Inantok na bigla si Ester, **pagkatapos** niyang uminom ng gatas.*
> *Sumama ang timpla ni Edwin, **pagkatapos** niyang mapanood ang sine.*
> *Humusay ang tenis ni Alberto, **pagkatapos** niyang kumuha ng lessons.*
> *Yumabang si Elvira, **pagkatapos** niyang pumasa sa Bar.*

Exercises

A. Supply appropriate temporal clauses as illustrated in the first item.

1. *Nagkasakit si Bernie,*
a. *buhat nang tumira siya sa bukid.* (Simultaneous start)
b. *habang tumitira siya sa bukid.* (Simultaneous ongoing)
c. *hanggang sa tumira siya sa bukid.* (Simultaneous termination)
d. *bago pa siya tumira sa bukid.* (Sequential)
e. *pagkatapos niyang tumira sa bukid.* (Reverse sequential)

2. *Nasipon si Jonathan,*
a.
b.
c.
d.
e.

3. *Humusay ang buhay ni Valdez,*
a.
b.
c.
d.
e.

4. *Magkasundung-magkasundo ang mag-asawa,*

a.

b.

c.

d.

e.

5. *Hindi nag-uusap ang magkapit-bahay,*

a.

b.

c.

d.

e.

B. Prepare to answer questions about the following temporal conjunctions.

1. *Gumanda ang tingin ni Jennifer sa buhay buhat nang makilala niya si Neal.*
2. *Nanlalaki ang mga mata ni Amado habang nagbibilang ng pera si Bob.*
3. *Hindi nakapanhik si Yoly, hanggang sa magkaanak siya.*
4. *Kataas na ng tingin kay Manny, bago pa siya naging doktor.*
5. *Nagsisi din si Crispin, pagkatapos niyang makulong.*

C. Answer the following questions based on the sentencex above.

1. *Kailan nagsimulang gumanda ang tingin ni Jennifer sa buhay?*

2. *Nakapanhik ba si Yoly bago siya nagkaanak?*

3. *Nagsisi din ba si Crispin? Kailan?*

4. *Ano ang nangyayari habang nagbibilang ng pera si Bob?*

5. *Naging doktor ba muna si Manny bago tumaas ang tingin sa kaniya?*

6. *Nakulong ba si Crispin bago siya nagsisi?*

7. *Nang nagkaanak si Yoly, nakapanhik din ba siya?*

8. *Bago pa lang nagbilang ng pera si Bob, nanlaki na ba ang mga mata ni Amado?*

9. *Dahil ba naging doktor si Manny kaya tumaas ang tingin sa kanya?*

10. *Maganda ba ang tingin ni Jennifer sa buhay nang hindi pa niya kilala si Neal?*

chapter 7

More on Conjoining

Clause Invertibility

In many conjunctions, the second clause, together with the conjunctor, may physically precede the first clause. For example:

Kumain ka ng marami, **para lumakas ka.**
Para lumakas ka, *kumain ka ng marami.*

Pumipito pa si Roger, **habang naglalakad.**
Habang naglalakad, *pumipito pa si Roger.*

Natulungan ko sana si Ben, **kung may magagawa lang sana ako.**
Kung may magagawa lang sana ako, *natulungan ko sana si Ben.*

Other conjunctions may not be inverted. For example:

Nalagas ang mga dahon, **at nalaglag ang mga bunga.**
***At nalaglag ang mga bunga,** *nalagas ang mga dahon.*

Kabata-bata pa ni Ramon, **pero maisip na siya.**
***Pero maisip na siya,** *kabata-bata pa ni Ramon.*

A third group of conjunctions allows inversion but only if both first and second clauses are introduced by conjunctors.

Binaha ang Maynila, **dahil sa** *umulan nang malakas.*
Dahil sa *umulan nang malakas* **kaya** *binaha ang Maynila.*

Huminto ang ulan, **at** *lumiwanag ang langit.*
At *lumiwanag ang langit,* **nang** *huminto ang ulan.*

139

The following is a list of conjunctors that allow or do not allow clause inversion.

Invertible	Non-Invertible
sa halip na, imbis na	at (saka, nang, etc.)
kahit	kaya (tuloy)
gayong	pero
bagama't	nguni't
kapag	datapwa't
kung	subali't
kung (saka-)sakali (man) (at)	gayun (pa) man
sa sandaling	o
(sa) oras na	o kaya
basta't	o kung hindi man
tuwing	samantala (contrast, counter-
sapul nang	assumption)
mula nang	at pagkatapos (sequential)
buhat nang	
buhat pa noong	
habang	
hanggang	
habang hindi	
bago (pa)	
samantalang (temporal)	
kaysa (sa)	

Conjunctors that allow inversion with optional or obligatory occurrence of conjunctors in the second clause.

> para ... (kaya)
> upang ... (kaya)
> nang ... (at saka)
> kung ... (at saka)
> pagkatapos (reverse sequential) ... (at saka)

> kasi...kaya
> dahil (sa, kasi) ... kaya
> papaano kasi ... kaya
> sapagka't ... kaya
> palibhasa'y ... kaya
> sa dahilan ... kaya

The following conjunctors are on the formal side and should be used rarely if at all in casual speech: bagama't, kung saka-sakali man at, sapul nang, samantalang, nguni't, subali't, datapwa't, gayon pa man, upang, sapagka't.

Exercises

a. Underline the clause that carries the conjunctor and determine its function (cause, effect, purpose, etc.).

1. *Manghingi ka kaya ng kamatis, o kaya, bumili ka na lang.*
2. *Kahit wala pa siyang pamilya, nagpagawa na siya ng bahay.*
3. *Mapapahiyaw siguro si Emma, oras na makita niya si Franco.*
4. *Bago nasira ang kotse, bumangga muna kami sa pader.*
5. *Imbis na tumakbo si Marcial, sumugod pa siya.*
6. *Ngayon at maluwag na ang buhay ni Annie, hindi na siya nakakak- ilala.*
7. *Uminom muna kayo ng kape, habang hindi pa dumarating si Esper.*
8. *Palibhasa'y ipinanganak na mayaman, hindi marunong magtrabaho si Igor.*
9. *Kalaking tao ni Martin, pero kaliit ng mga paa niya.*
10. *Para humaba ang buhay mo, magkakain ka ng yogurt.*

b. Supply component clauses.

1. *Habang*   ,
2. *Kahit*   ,
3.   *, at pagkatapos*
4.   *, gayong*
5. *Tuwing*   ,
6.   *, o*
7. *Kung*   ,
8. *Dahil sa*   ,
9.   *, kasi*
10.   *, buhat nang*

Transition Phrases and Introducer Clauses

Transition words, phrases, and clauses connect the ideas expressed in a series of sentences. Like conjunctors, these transition devices, along with certain particles, insure the continuity of the flow of ideas through the discourse. Although only transition clauses result in complex sentences, we present all three here because of their functional affinity with conjunctors.

Alalaong baga (ay)   In other words
Alalaong baga'y bumuti na siya.
Alalaong baga, dapat mo siyang ipagtanggol

(Ang) akala ko ba (ay)   I thought
Akala ko ba'y umuwi ka sa Pilipinas.
Akala ko ba'y nasa Hawaii ka.

Ang tutuo (nito) (ay)   The truth of the matter is
Ang tutuo, naubusan na rin ako ng pera.
Ang tutuo nito'y gusto ko na ring tumutol.

(At) isa pa   (And) one more thing
Isa pa, mahusay din naman siyang tatay.
At isa pa, may sasakyan si Debra.

(At) sa wakas   (And) finally; At last
Sa wakas, umandar na rin ang kotse.
At sa wakas, may tagapagtanggol na rin kami.

Bago ko malimutan   Before I forget
Bago ko malimutan, nakita mo ba si Jonathan sa miting?
Bako ko malimutan, pupunta ba kayo sa amin bukas?

E   Well; And
E ano ang sinabi mo?
E si John yata ang kumuha.

Gayun (pa) man (ay)   Nevertheless; Be that as it may
Gayunman, hindi pa rin nanalo si Tatoo.
Gayunma'y mahalaga pa rin siya sa akin.

Halimbawa   For example
Halimbawa, kumbinsihin muna natin si Dado.
Halimbawa, isa-isa tayong bumati kay Annie.

Ipagpalagay na natin na Let's assume that
Ipagpalagay na natin na nasira ang preno ng kotse.
Ipagpalagay na natin na hindi siya darating bukas.

Kalabas-labas nito (ay) The end result of all of this
Kalabas-labas nito, ako pa ang may kasalanan.
Kalabas-labas nito, ikaw pa ang sisisihin.

Kamukat-mukat ko When I came to my senses
Kakita-kita ko I just happened to see
Kadinig-dinig ko I just happened to hear
Kabali-balita ko I just happened to hear the news
Kamukat-mukat ko, nakatakbo na siya.
Kadinig-dinig ko, nasa Amerika na pala si Ernesto.

Kahit manawari (ay) May it be that
Kahit manawari'y manalo ka sana.
Kahit manawari, makita mo ang hinahanap mo.

Kapagdaka (ay) All of a sudden
Kapagdaka'y sumibad siya ng takbo.
Kapagdaka, inihagis niya ang radyo sa ilog.

Kasi (ay) The reason is, It's because
Kasi'y napakabilis mong magmaneho.
Kasi, hindi mo iniisip ang ginagawa mo.

Kasabi-sabi (ba naman) ay (He) carelessly said
Kasabi-sabi ba nama'y hindi ka raw tumutulong sa bahay.

Katanung-tanong (ba naman) (ay) (He) carelessly asked
Katanung-tanong ba naman, kaanu-ano daw ba kita?

Katunayan (ay) In fact
Katunayan, mahusay pa ang andar ng kotse.
Katunaya'y nagpapart-time ako tuwing Sabado.

Kung gayon (ay) Therefore
Kung gayon, nagkakaintindihan pala tayo.
Kung gayo'y hindi ka pa pala nag-uumpisa.

Kung sa bagay After all
Kung sa bagay, malaki naman ang kinikita niya.
Kung sa bagay, marami siyang kilala sa City Hall.

Kung tutuusin (ay)   To sum it all up
Kung tutuusin, hindi siya dapat magdamdam.
Kung tutuusi'y malaki rin naman ang hirap niya.

Maalaala ko nga pala   Come to remember it
Maisip-isip ko nga pala   Come to think of it
Maalaala ko nga pala, wala bang ipinagbilin si Felipe?
Maisip-isip ko nga pala, hindi ba't darating si Miska bukas?

Malao't madali (ay)   Sooner or later
Malao't madali'y magkakamali din siya.
Malao't madali, babagsak din siya sa mga kamay ko.

Mangyari (ay)   The reason is
Mangyari'y kulang pa ako sa ekspiriyensiya.
Mangyari, wala na akong magawa.

Ngayon   Now
Ngayon, ibuhos mo na ang patis.
Ngayon, gagawa tayo ng isang malaking kasinungalingan.

Palibhasa (ay)   It's because
Palibhasa'y malaki ang galit mo kay Marco.
Palibhasa, walang pinag-aralan si Martin.

Sa madaling salita (ay)   In other words
Sa madaling salita'y nalugi si Daniel.
Sa madaling salita, sumira siya sa kanyang pangako.

Samakatuwid (ay)   Therefore
Samakatuwid ay hindi mo alam magmaneho.
Samakatuwid, may pag-asa pa tayong umani nang malaki.

Samatala (ay)   Meanwhile
Samantala, sa rantso ay nagkagalit ang mag-asawa.
Samantala'y inuna muna ni Miguel ang sarili niya.

Siyanga pala   By the way
Siyanga pala, kilala mo ba si Jasmin?
Siyanga pala, kailangan palang bumili ako ng matamis.

Teka muna (at)   Wait a minute
Teka muna, tatawag lang ako sa bahay.
Teka muna't iinom muna ako ng kape.

One thing to remember about transition clauses is that when an actor is called for, it is nontopic.

Akala **ko** ba	not	*Akala **ako** ba
Bago **ko** malimutan	not	*Bako **ako** malimutan
		(But, bago **ako** makalimut)
Kamukat-mukat **ko**	not	*Kamukat-mukat **ako**
Kakita-kita **ko**	not	*Kakita-kita **ako**
Maalaala **ko** nga pala	not	*Maalaala **ako** nga pala
etc.		

Exercises

a. Match the Tagalog and English transition elements.

1. Halimbawa	a.	After all
2. Sa madaling salita	b.	Nevertheless
3. Samantala	c.	Now
4. Isa pa	d.	For example
5. Sa wakas	e.	At last; Finally
6. Ipagpalagay na natin	f.	Meanwhile
7. Samakatuwid	g.	In other words
8. Kung sa bagay	h.	Let us assume that
9. Ngayon	i.	Another thing
10. Gayunman	j	Therefore

b. Translate into Tagalog.

1. By the way, are you going any place tomorrow?

2. After all, you never liked the movie, did you?

3. Meanwhile, the police searched his apartment.

4. The truth of the matter is that John is going broke.

5. Therefore, we will send a delegation to the President.

6. Well, didn't you stop him?

7. And what did you do at school today?

8. And one more thing, you will stop smoking.

9. In fact, I have your confession right here.

Changes on the Clauses

Conjoining typically requires no more than joining two simple sentences with a conjunctor. Some combinations, however, require certain changes to be made in the clauses. Two important changes will be discussed, namely, pronoun formation and conjunction reduction.

Pronoun Formation

When joining the simple sentences in (a) below to express a counter-assumption, the correct sentence is (c) and not (b).

    a. *Malakas pa si Manuel. Matanda na si Manuel.*
    b. **Malakas pa rin **si Manuel** kahit matanda na **si Manuel**.*
    c. *Malakas pa rin si Manuel kahit matanda na **siya**.*

That is, you would change the second occurrence of *si Manuel* to its pronoun equivalent *siya* 'he / she.' This is pronoun formation. Other examples:

    *Nawala **si Dindo**, kaya nagtanong **siya**.*
    *Dumaan sa tindahan **si Pepe**, bago **siya** umuwi.*
    *Umuwi na **si Oscar**, dahil pagod na **siya**.*

Pronoun formation depends on the condition that the nouns have the same referrent. The second noun *must* be replaced by the equivalent pronoun, or else the listener will think it refers to a different object.

Exercise

Underline the constituents with the same referrent in the following sentences.

Example: *Nagkasala si Serafin kaya humingi siya ng tawad.*

1. *Maghapon sa trabaho si Mando, kaya pagod siya.*
2. *Magdamag kumanta ang mga bata, kaya minamalat sila.*
3. *Uminom muna ng alak si Levy, para dumulas ang dila niya.*
4. *Napahampas ang kotse ni Mario sa poste, at pagkatapos, bumangga ito sa pader.*
5. *Madaling turuan si Leila, pero madali lang siyang makalimot.*

6. *Imbis na pumunta sa Maynila si Dorian, nag-side trip siya sa Laguna.*

7. *Kumaway ba si Amanda, o kinamot lang niya ang ulo niya?*

8. *Sumilip muna sa pinto si Ivan, bago siya kumatok.*

The choice of pronoun depends on the *function, number,* and *person* of the noun phrase.

The functions are either *subject* or *nonsubject,* and if nonsubject, either *oblique* or *nonoblique.* The oblique function, for the purpose of this section, denotes object of prepositions.

The following chart should guide you in the selection of the correct pronoun form.

Subject Pronouns		
Person	**Singular**	**Plural**
First	*ako*	*kami* (exclusive)
		tayo (inclusive)
Second	*ikaw*	*kayo* (plural)
Third	*siya*	*sila*

Non-Subject, Non-Oblique Pronouns		
Person	**Singular**	**Plural**
First	*ko*	*amin* (exclusive)
		natin (inclusive)
Second	*mo*	*ninyo*
Third	*niya*	*nila*

Non-Subject, Non-Oblique Pronouns		
Person	**Singular**	**Plural**
First	*akin*	*amin* (exclusive)
		atin (inclusive)
Second	*iyo*	*inyo*
Third	*kaniya*	*kanila*

The words in bold in the first set of sentences below are subject phrases. They are replaced by subject pronouns in the sentences on the right.

Sumakay **ang mga bata** sa kalabaw.   Sumakay **sila** sa kalabaw.
Sumulat **si Nina** ng kuwento.   Sumulat **siya** ng kuwento.

These same phrases are non-subject, non-oblique phrases in the sentences below. They are replaced by pronouns with the same function.

Sinakyan **ng mga bata** ang kalabaw.   Sinakyan **nila** ang kalabaw.
Sinulat **ni Nina** ang kuwento.   Sinulat **niya** ang kuwento.

In the next set of sentences, the noun phrases in bold are non-subject, oblique phrases, which are replaced by pronouns with the same function. The pronouns are preceded by the oblique marker *sa*.

Sumulat si Dante **kay Miss Perlas.**   Sumulat si Dante **sa kaniya.**
Pumikit si Danilo **sa mga dalaga.**   Pumikit si Danilo **sa kanila.**

Person refers to the familiar categories of first person, second person, and third person. Number is singular or plural. In Tagalog, the first person plural pronouns differ between those that include the listener and those that exclude the listener.

To repeat the rule on forming a pronoun in conjunctions: if a noun in the second conjunct has the same referent as a noun in the first conjunct, it must be replaced by its pronoun equivalent. The choice of pronoun form is determined by the function, number, and person of the antecedent phrase.

Exercise

The pronoun in the second clause incorrectly matches its antecedent. Replace the pronoun with the correct form.

1. *Natulog nang maaga* **si Evita**, *para maaga* **niyang** *magising.*
2. *Nanunuod ng TV* **si Gilda**, *habang nakikipag-usap* **ko** *sa telepono.*
3. *Pinakain* **mo** *na sa palad, kinagat* **tayo** *pa.*
4. *Nakapasa* **si Maggie** *sa interview, kaya napakasaya* **siya.**
5. *Tuwing magkikita* **si Oscar at Cecile** *sa lobby, nagngingitian* **siya.**

6. *Sinundo **nila** si Ben sa airport, at saka dinala **niya** sa hotel.*
7. *Sinundo nila **si Ben** sa airport, at saka dinala **niya** sa hotel.*
8. *Tumakbo **ka** sa tindahan at bumili **kayo** ng gatas.*
9. *Hindi aasenso **si Diego**, kasi masyado **akong** tahimik.*
10. *Tanggapin **mo** na kahit anong trabaho, habang naghihintay **mo**.*

There can be more than one potential antecedent. In the example below, the form "X" can refer to either Derek or Marvin. What should the form of "X" be?

Sinuntok ni Derek si Marvin bago "X" umalis.

The form depends on whether the antecedent is an actor or a non-actor phrase. If the antecedent is actor, a pronoun is used, otherwise the demonstrative equivalent is used (this rule has exceptions). In (a) below the pronoun *siya* refers to the actor phrase Derek; in (b) the demonstrative *ito* refers to the patient phrase Marvin.

a. *Sinuntok ni Derek si Marvin bago **siya** (si Derek) umalis.*
b. *Sinuntok ni Derek si Marvin bago **ito** (si Marvin) umalis.*

Similarly:

Sumulat si Derek kay Marvin bago siya (si Derek) umalis.
Sumulat si Derek kay Marvin bago ito (si Marvin) umalis.

The demonstrative pronoun *ito* is subject. Its nonsubject counterpart is *nito*.

Study the following sentences.

Inutusan ni Mario si Dindo, habang nagpapahinga ito (si Dindo).
Pinuwersa ni Digna si Esper, para umamin ito (si Esper).
Pumanig pa rin si Martin kay Daniel, gayong inamin nito (Daniel) ang kasalanan.
Minasama ni Bob si Ian, samantalang napakabait nito (si Ian).

Exercise

Supply the appropriate pronoun. The antecedent is in bold.

1. *Nginitian ni Amor **si Marco**, para naman maligayahan (?)*
2. *Tumulong si Ruben **kay Isram**, para matapos ang trabaho (?)*
3. *Humingi **si Perla** ng sigarilyo kay Dory, dahil naubusan (?)*
4. *Pinainitan muna ni Ron **ang garapon**, bago niya binuksan (?)*
5. *Habang pinangangaralan ni Dante **si Minda**, tatangu-tango lang naman (?)*
6. *Malaki rin ang naitulong **ni Helen** kay Paul, bago (?) umalis.*
7. *Tinukso na naman ni Paul **si Regina**, kaya mainit ang ulo (?).*
8. *Sinagot nang malakas ni Mario **si Leilani**, kaya masama ang loob (?).*
9. *Itinulak ni Mannie **si Bert**, para hindi (?) mahagip ng kotse.*
10. *Sinamahan **ni Ramon** si Alicia sa tindahan, dahil gusto (?) makausap ito.*

Conjunction Reduction

Another way to make a sentence like (a) below acceptable, other than replacing the second noun with its pronoun equivalent, is to simply delete the second noun, as in sentence (c). This is conjunction reduction.

a. **Malakas pa rin **si Manuel** kahit matanda na **si Manuel**.*
b. *Malakas pa rin **si Manuel** kahit matanda na **siya**.*
c. *Malakas pa rin **si Manuel** kahit matanda na.*

Conjunction reduction also depends on the idea of "same referrent." A noun phrase of the second clause may be dropped if it has the same referrent as a noun phrase in the first clause. Here are other examples:

Naghilamos si Estelita, bago natulog.
Nagtrabaho si Perla, imbis na maglibang-libang.
Kumakanta pa si Angela, habang nagluluto.

Exercise

Restore the deleted phrase in the second clause.

Example:
>   *Dati'y malapit si Inday, pero ngayon malayo na.*
>   *...pero ngayon malayo na **si Inday**.*

1. *Ayaw magkakain ni Tarcila kaya tuloy namamayat.*
2. *Lumundag sa tuwa si Oscar, at hag-sirko pa!*
3. *Gayong tinitigan lang si Norine ng asawa niya, nagkaanak na.*
4. *Laging ngumingiti si Roberto, buhat nang manggaling sa dentista.*
5. *Napahampas ang kotse ni Mario sa poste, at pagkatapos, napabangga pa sa pader.*
6. *Pinunit muna ni Satur ang sulat ni Cely, bago itinapon.*
7. *Nagpa-face lift si Mely, para raw bumata.*
8. *Kakain ka ba o manunuod ng TV?*
9. *Sumulat ka kay Terry, at nang maalaala ka naman.*
10. *Sa halip na purihin ni Mike si Elizabeth, pinintasan pa (2 phrases).*

It appears that in all cases where the second noun phrase can be replaced by a pronoun, it can also be deleted.

>   *Maghapon sa trabaho si Amado, kaya pagod **siya**.* (pronominalization)
>   *Maghapon sa trabaho si Amado, kaya pagod.* (reduction)

>   *Uminom ng alak si Levy, para dumulas ang dila **niya**.*
>   *Uminom ng alak si Levy, para dumulas ang dila.*

>   *Sumilip muna sa pinto si Igor, bago **siya** kumatok.*
>   *Sumilip muna sa pinto si Igor, bago kumatok.*

In sentences with more than one potential antecedent, the deleted pronoun is assumed to refer to the subject of the first clause.

>   *Nagtanong si Derek kay Marvin, bago siya umalis.*
>   *Nagtanong si Derek kay Marvin, bago umalis.*   (si Derek)

Tinanong ni Derek si Marvin, bago ito umalis.
Tinanong ni Derek si Marvin bago umalis.   *(si Marvin)*

It is not uncommon to have in the second clause both a pronoun and a demonstrative. The pronoun still refers to the actor, and the demonstrative to the non-actor nominal.

Sinuntok ni Derek si Marvin, bago niya (Derek) pinaalis ito (Marvin).
Sinuntok ni Derek si Marvin, bago siya (Derek) pinaalis nito (Marvin).

In these sentences, the demonstrative or the pronoun or both may be deleted.

Sinuntok ni Derek si Marvin, bago niya pinaalis.
Sinuntok ni Derek si Marvin, bago siya pinaalis.
Sinuntok ni Derek si Marvin, bago pinaalis.

How about a sentence with *three* potential antecedents in the first clause?

Pinasuntok ni Bob si Bill kay John bago siya umalis.
Pinasuntok ni Bob si Bill kay John bago ito umalis.

Pinasuntok ni Bob si Bill kay John bago siya pinaalis nito.
Pinasuntok ni Bob si Bill kay John bago niya pinaalis ito.

To understand these sentences, the simplest strategy is to request for clarification, for example, *Sino ang umalis?* 'Who left?'

chapter 8

Complex Sentences: Embedding

In the last two chapters, we look at how, by joining one simple sentence after another, complex sentences are formed. In this chapter, we look at another way of combining simple sentences – embedding.

Embedding

While conjoining joins sentences, *embedding*, on the other hand, inserts a sentence into a component of another sentence. Observe how it is done. First, here are two simple sentences:

> *Isinulat ko ang balita kay Ben.*   I wrote the news to Ben.
> *Dumating si Jim.*   Jim arrived.

The second sentence can be made a part of the subject phrase *ang balita* of the first sentence.

> *Isinulat ko **ang balita na dumating si Jim** kay Ben.*

The word *balita* serves as the headword to which the embedded sentence is attached using the linker *na.* The embedded sentence serves as a modification of this headword, restricting its meaning.

What defines embedding is the relegation of the embedded sentence into a sub-part of a constituent of the host sentence.

153

In the examples below, the embedded sentences, or what's left of them, are in bold letters. The linkers are underlined. Notice the absence of a headword in the last sentence.

> Hinuli ng pulis ang trabahador <u>na</u> **nanira ng monumento.**
> Ginasta ni Mario ang pera<u>ng</u> **naipon ni Susan.**
> Pinaniwalaan ni Dexter <u>na</u> **babalik si Perla.**

Exercises

a. Which sentences are examples of conjoining and which are embedding?

1. Nalito si Mike at nasiraan naman ng loob si Don.

2. Inulan ang Maynila, at nilindol pa.

3. Maganda ang babaeng nakaupo sa pasigan.

4. Mapurol ang gulok na binili ni Max.

5. Sumama ang sikmura ni Joe, pero magaling na siya.

6. Tinanong si Dexter kung ayos na siya.

7. Inubos ni Jodi ang cake, kaya umatungal si Nini.

8. Ayaw ni Guy na uminom ng murang alak.

9. Kailangang magluto tayo ng patatas para sa bisiting puti.

10. Nalutas na rin ang pag-iyak-iyak ni Amanda.

b. Underline the embedded clauses, circle the linker (if shown), and cross out the headword (if any).

1. Umilag kayo sa mga taong madulas ang dila.

2. Iwasan ang pagsasabi ng masama sa kapwa.

3. Narinig ni Ester ang bulungan na aalis siya.

4. Gusto ni Manuel na magpalista si Marco sa U.S. Navy.

5. Nawala sa ulo ni David ang bagay na malakas maghilik si Rosa.

6. Pinag-usapan sa klase ang bintang na espiya siya.

7. Narinig ni Leon na wala raw takot si Edgar.

8. *Ipinipilit ni Pierre na masaya ang mga Pinoy.*

9. *Tama ba ang pagtawa ni Dindo sa mali ni Dolores?*

10. *Lumusong sila sa balong sila rin ang humukay.*

c. Complete these sentences by supplying an embedded clause.

1. *Sinagap ni Johnny ang balita na*

2. *Papaano ba ang pag-*

3. *Sino ba ang babaeng*

4. *Si Martin ang taong*

5. *Hinamon ni Carlos si Pepe na*

The Function of Embedding

The embedded sentence adds a piece of information about a constituent of the host sentence. The embedded clause may make the meaning of the headword more specific. This is shown in the following example, where the embedded clause *inakyat ni Ben* limits the meaning of the headword *papaya*.

> *Tinalupan ni Helga ang papayang **inakyat ni Ben.***

When the headword is an "empty" word, for example, *bagay* 'thing', *balita* 'news', *tao* 'one, someone', etc., it may be deleted.

> *Hinuli ng pulis ang (taong) sumira ng monumento.*

Exercise

Determine the embedded clauses in the following English sentences.

1. Pete advised Mary to behave herself.
2. Sue claims that the world will end tomorrow.
3. Desmond shot the man who made fun of his pacifist theory.
4. I believe that the world will be a better place to live in.

5. He who stumbles will fail.
6. The shooting of the pandas was denounced in the press.
7. Stiff neck is a condition that afflicts avid graffiti readers.
8. I want you to go.
9. I never wanted to go.

When a sentence is embedded in another, it becomes a part of it, performing a particular grammatical function. It may function as a nominal, or as a modifier of a nominal.

The Embedded Clause as a Nominal

As a nominal, the embedded clause is typically the subject of the sentence. In a few cases it can be the object of the verb. And unlike regular nominals, it cannot serve as a predicate, nor can it serve as an object of prepositions.

The Nominal Clause as Subject   Not all verbs can take a sentential subject. Three classes of verbs that do are pseudo-verbs, verbs of perception, and verbs of reporting.

Subject of Pseudo-Verbs

*Ayaw ni Oscar na **humingi ng tulong si Clarisa**.*
*Gusto ni Marco na **uminom ng gamot si Susan**.*
*Alam ni Marsha na **sinungaling si Joseph**.*
*Ibig ni Daniel na **umuwi nang maaga si Erika**.*

How do we know that the embedded clauses function as subject? (Try replacing them with pronouns.)

The so-called modals are similar to pseudo-verbs in this respect. They may also take subject clauses, and a subject pronoun can likewise be substituted for this clause. Opinions differ, however, as to whether these sentences have simple or complex structures.

Subject of Modal Verbs

Dapat na **umalis ka na**.
Maaaring **mabuhay pa ang halaman**.
Baka **mag-istrayk na naman ang mga drayber**.
Puwedeng **humabol pa si Mario kay Eddie**.
Tutuong **napakaganda ng gabi sa bundok**.

Tunay na **magaganda ang mga tanim ni Aretha**.
Tila **iiyak na naman si Anne**.

Exercises

a. Underline the embedded clause in each of the following.

1. *Kailangan ni John na tumestigo si Paul.*

2. *Gusto ni Lauro na pumunta sa New York.*

3. *Ibig ni Martin na magsaka na lang.*

4. *Kaya ni Michael na languyin ang English Channel.*

5. *Alam ni Judith na mangingisda si Simon.*

b. Respond with a sentence whose subject is an embedded clause.

1. *Ano ang ayaw gawin ni Dexter?*
   Ayaw ni Dexter na maglaro ng tenis sa tanghali.

2. *Ano ang kayang gawin ni Derek?*

3. *Ano ang ibig kunin ni Sally?*

4. *Ano ang kailangang bilhin ni Rudy?*

5. *Ano ang gustong gawin ni Miriam?*

6. *Ano ang ibig mangyari ng Presidente?*

7. *Ano ang alam kumpunihin ng Lolo?*

8. *Ano ang ibig basahin ni Clint?*

9. *Ano ang ayaw gawin ni Romualdo?*

10. *Ano ang ibig mangyari ni John?*

c. List five things that you *should* do.

1. *Dapat (na)*

2. *Dapat (na)*

3. *Kailangan(g)*

4. *Kailangan(g)*

5. *Dapat (na)*

d. Using pseudo-modals, give the Tagalog opposites of the following prohibitions.

1. No trespassing at night.
2. No parking on Sundays.
3. No littering on the street.
4. No smoking.
5. No swimming in the dark.

e. Give five events or conditions that are generally true.

1. *Tutuong maginaw ang Pasko sa Canada.*
2. *Tunay na*
3.
4.
5.

f. List five speculations on world events.

Example: *Baka makipagkasundo si Castro sa Amerika.*

1. *Baka*
2. *Tila*
3.
4.
5.

Subject of Verbs of Perception Verbs of perception refer to sensing or perceiving. Some examples are:

nakita	seen	*natikman*	tasted
naamoy	smelled	*narinig*	heard
napansin	noticed	*naisip*	thought
nalasahan	tasted	*naino*	noticed
namatyagan	noticed	*nasilip*	seen
naulinigan	heard	*napanaginipan*	dreamt
naramdaman	felt		

The sentence subjects are underlined in the following examples.

> **Naamoy** *ni Tarcila na <u>nasusunog ang pizza</u>.*
> **Narinig** *ni Donna na <u>tinamaan ng kidlat si Miguel sa paa</u>.*
> **Nakita** *ng pasahero na <u>iniligtas ng drayber ang babae</u>.*
> **Nalasahan** *ni Marcial na <u>maasim ang sinigang</u>.*

Subject of Verbs of Reporting   Verbs of reporting state the way a clause is expressed or communicated. They, too, may take on sentential subjects. Some examples:

sinabi	said	*ibinalita*	reported
itinatwa	denied	*ibinulong*	whispered
isinulat	wrote	*ikinalat*	spread word around
binanggit	mentioned	*ibinunyag*	revealed
pinabulaanan	denied	*idinaldal*	spread word around
isinigaw	shouted	*ipinilit*	insisted
pinatutuhanan	confirmed	*ipinagkaila*	denied

> **Sinabi** *ni Daniel na <u>mamimili siya sa downtown</u>.*
> **Binaggit** *ni Sophia na <u>makikipag-usap siya kay Carlo</u>.*
> **Isinulat** *ni Ramon na <u>maluwag na ang buhay sa Pilipinas</u>.*
> **Ipinagkaila** *ni Martina na <u>kinontak siya ng KGB kahapon</u>.*

In general, and in contrast to the class of sentences with pseudo-verbs, sentences with verbs of perception and reporting do not necessarily trigger deletion of a coreferential noun in the lower clause. The nominals in bold below are coreferential, but deletion of the pronoun is not allowed.

> *Sinabi ni **Danny** na mamimili **siya** sa downtown.*
> *Napanaginipan ni **Joaquin** na nalugi **siya** sa negosyo.*
> *Narinig ni **Marsha** na pinulaan **siya** ni Regina.*

Exercises

a. Complete the following sentences with one of these verbs: *naamoy, narinig, nakita, nabalitaan.*

1.   *ni Marcia na dumarating si Amanda.*

2.   *ni David na umugong ang eroplano.*

3.   *ni Bill na humalimuyak ang pabango.*

4.   *ni Fernando na darating daw si Sophia.*

b. Complete the following sentences with an embedded clause.

1. *Naramdaman ni Manuel na*
2. *Napansin ni Yvonne na*
3. *Naisip ni Joel na*
4. *Ibinulong ni Gina na*
5. *Itinatwa ni Barbara na*

c. Respond to the following questions as shown in the example.

Example:
   Q: *Ano ang naramdaman ni Magno?*
   A: *Naramdaman ni Magno na sumakit ang ulo niya.*

1. *Ano ang naulinigan ni Benigno?*
2. *Ano ang itinatwa ni Amanda?*
3. *Ano ang isinigaw ni Charlie?*
4. *Ano ang nakita ni Blas?*
5. *Ano ang narinig ni Basil?*
6. *Ano ang sinabi ng kartero?*
7. *Ano ang ibinalita ng announcer?*
8. *Ano ang sinabi niya?*
9. *Ano ang ibinulong ni Clint?*
10. *Ano ang nasilip ni Divina?*

The Nominal Clause as Object   A few verbs have forms that allow the embedded clause to be object: *nanaginip, naniwala, nagpasabi, nagbilin, nagpilit, nagkaila, bumulong.*

Nanaginip *si Ismael na <u>dumami ang baka niya</u>.*
Nagpasabi *si Gina na <u>kakain siya ng hapunan dito</u>.*
Nagbilin *si Hagar na <u>uuwi siya sa Sabado</u>.*
Naniwala *si Helga na <u>maagang matatapos ang Winter</u>.*

In general, the verb forms that take clauses as subjects are the more commonly used.

Exercises

a. Underline the embedded clause and determine whether it is the subject or object.

1. *Napansin ni Gaston na humihina ang katawan niya.*
2. *Itinatwa ni Marvin na naibangga niya ang kotse.*
3. *Naniwala si Greg na mahal ang bilihin sa Honolulu.*
4. *Isinulat ni Pierre na mahirap ang buhay sa Paris.*
5. *Nagpasabi si Emmanuel na magdala ka ng mga CDs sa party.*
6. *Naisip ni Mathias na mag-invest sa mga antiques.*
7. *Nabasa ni Larry na mainit sa Las Vegas kung summer.*
8. *Sumulat ang Tatay na magaan na raw ang buhay sa Pilipinas.*
9. *Naniwala ang pari na walang kasalanan ang babae.*
10. *Pinilit ng nars na inumin ni Marcela ang pampatulog.*

b. Change the following sentences so that the embedded clause is the subject.

1. *Sumulat si Percy na hinihintay ka niya sa L.A.*
2. *Bumulong si Benson na kailangan niya ang kotse mamaya.*
3. *Nagpilit si Scotty na nanunuod si Angela ng classical movies.*
4. *Naniwala ang Nanay na marunong nang magluto si Cecille.*
5. *Nagpasabi ang boss ko na hindi siya papasok sa trabaho.*

c. Embed the following clauses as subjects.

1. *Dakila ang ninuno niya.*
2. *Pupunta ako sa bayan bukas.*
3. *Malulusaw na ang snow.*
4. *Nagustuhan na rin niya ang pagkaing Pilipino.*
5. *Hindi siya komportableng makipag-usap sa telepono.*

The Embedded Nominalized Clause

The focus of a clause may be shifted from a noun phrase to the verb, which undergoes a change in form and becomes nominalized. The clause then functions as a noun. The most common nominalizing prefix is *pag-*. Observe how it is done.

> Sentence: *Bumili si Marta ng gamot.*
> Nominalized clause: *Ang **pag**bili ni Marta ng gamot...*

The subject in the original clause loses its subject marker: *si Marta* becomes *ni Marta*. The verb loses its focus and the nominalizing prefix *pag-* is attached to the root: *bumili* becomes *pagbili*. Other examples:

> *Kumuha ang boksingero ng leksiyon.*
>   *Ang **pag**kuha ng boksingero ng leksiyon...*
> *Sumama si Thelma sa kanya.*
>   *Ang **pag**sama ni Thelma sa kanya...*
> *Sumama ang loob ni Francisco.*
>   *Ang **pag**sama ng loob ni Francisco...*
> *Umulan nang malakas.*
>   *Ang **pag**-ulan nang malakas...*

Nominalized clauses appear in the usual positions occupied by noun phrases: subject phrase, non-subject non-oblique phrase (introduced by *ng*), non-subject oblique phrase (introduced by *sa*), and predicate.

As Subject Clause
*Ipinagkaila ni Gina **ang pagpunta niya sa bar**.*
*Nabalita sa buong bayan **ang pagdalaw ni Miriam kay Ben**.*
*Nakita ko mismo **ang pagbagsak ng bubong ng bahay**.*
*Napansin din ng Nanay **ang pag-iyak ni Mike**.*

As Non-Subject Non-Oblique Clause
*Ginulat si Yuki **ng paglundag ni Akihiro sa bakod**.*
*Binagabag ang sanggol **ng pag-ingit ng pinto**.*
*Inabala ang drayber **ng paghinto ng kotse sa harapan ng bus**.*
*Sinalubong si Michael **ng pag-iyak ni Mindi**.*

As Non-Subject Oblique Clause
*Humusay si Joaquin **sa pagtugtog ng ukelele**.*
*Humanga si Bernie **sa paghabi ng kasinungalingan ni Brenda**.*
*Tumulong ang pulis **sa pagtawid ng matanda**.*
*Umilag si Daisy **sa pagtayo ni Edgar**.*

Nominalized Clause as Predicate   A noun may serve as predicate of the sentence, for example, **Sundalo** si Amado. A nominalized clause may also serve as predicate. However, it requires that its subject must also be a clause. In the first example below, the nominal predicate ang pagkanta ni Ismael is followed by the subject ang gumulat sa bata, which is an embedded clause.

Ang pagkanta ni Ismael ang gumulat sa bata.
Ang pag-inom ni Crispin nang marami ang sumira sa party.
Ang pagbilang ni Carla nang mali ang ikinagalit ng customer.
Ang pagkatok niya sa pinto ang bumulahaw kay Fred.

Exercises

a.   Transform the following sentences into nominalized clauses.

1.   *Lumundag si Akihiro sa bakod.*

2.   *Kumain ang bisita ng sinangag.*

3.   *Sumulat si Oscar sa Presidente.*

4.   *Humiwalay si Mariano kay Jasmine.*

5.   *Humina ang katawan ng matandang pari.*

b.   Form sentences such that your answers in the previous exercise serve as

1.   the subject of an embedded sentence

2.   a phrase introduced by *ng*

3.   a phrase introduced by *sa*

4.   predicate

The prefix *pag-* is one of four nominalizing prefixes. The choice of form depends on the form of the source verb. The chart below shows the different combinations.

Nominalizing Prefixes		
Verb Class	Prefix	Example
-um-	pag-	pagdala
ma-	pagka-	pagka(ka)bili
mag-	pag-	pagkuha
mang-	pang-	panghihingi

Some examples:

Sentence:	*Uminom si Damian ng gamot.*
Nominalized Clause:	*Ang pag-inom ni Damian ng gamot ...*

Sentence:	*Nabili ni Damian ang bahay.*
Nominalized Clause:	*Ang pagka(ka)bili ni Damian sa bahay ...*

Sentence:	*Nagdala si Damian ng inumin.*
Nominalized Clause:	*Ang pagdala ni Damian ng inumin ...*

Sentence:	*Nanghingi si Damian ng tubig.*
Nominalized Clause:	*Ang panghihingi ni Damian ng tubig ...*

Exercise

Transform the following basic sentences into nominalized clauses.

1. *Kumuha si Dan ng mga bato sa pasigan.*
2. *Binuksan ni Marvin ang bintana.*
3. *Nadala ng pulis ang passport ko.*
4. *Namimitas sila ng mga bulaklak tuwing umaga.*
5. *Nagtinda si Manny ng diyaryo sa parke.*
6. *Nabangga ng motorsiklo ang matandang babae.*
7. *Nangutngot sila ng patatas sa likodbahay.*
8. *Nagtapon si Leonora ng mga lumang damit.*
9. *Nangalap ang mga scouts ng mga lumang diyaryo.*
10. *Pinansin ni Nina ang bagong damit ni Leticia.*

There is a difference between a *nominal* clause and a *nominalized* clause. The nominal clause is a basic sentence unchanged in the process of embedding.

Sentence:	*Bumili si Jimmy ng alak.*
Nominal Clause:	*Sinabi ni Rosie na **bumili si Jimmy ng alak.***

On the other hand, the nominalized clause undergoes changes in embedding.

Sentence:	*Bumili si Jimmy ng alak.*
Nominalized Clause:	*Itinatwa ni Rosie **ang pagbili ni Jimmy ng alak.***

The nominal clause occurs mainly as subject of the sentence, and, in a few cases, as "object" of *ng* (that is to say, in non-subject non-oblique position). The nominalized clause performs a wider range of noun functions: subject, oblique and non-oblique phrases, and predicate.

The Embedded Clause as a Nominal Expansion

The embedded clause may serve to modify a head noun. It restricts the range of referrents of the head noun. In the first example below, the clause *nanghuli ng isda sa akwaryum* limits the referrent of *tao* 'man.'

Hinanap ng mga pulis ang taong nanghuli ng isda sa akwaryum.
Itinatwa ni Oscar ang balita na hinuli ng pulis si Regina.

These examples illustrate two types of clause modifiers. In the first example, the head noun *tao* is an argument of the verb *nanghuli* of the embedded clause. The clause is called a relative clause. In the second example, the head noun *balita* is not an argument of the verb *hinuli* of the embedded clause. The clause serves as a complement of the noun.

Noun Complement

Only a small set of nouns can serve as the head noun in this construction: *bagay*, *balita*, and words functionally synonymous with *balita*, such as *sabi-sabi*, *bulung-bulungan*, *kuwento*, *sekreto*, and others.

Study the following examples. Isolate the head noun and the clause modifier.

> *Ikinalat ni Jasmine ang balita na ikakasal siya sa Hunyo.*
> *Narinig ko ang sabi-sabi na mag-aasawa uli si Gilda.*
> *Ikinaila ng gobyerno ang balita na may eleksyon sa Nobyembre.*

When the headword is deleted, the result is the same sentence as the first type of embedding we discussed.

> *Ikinalat ni Jasmine na ikakasal siya sa Hunyo.*
> *Narinig ko na mag-aasawa uli si Gilda.*
> *Ikinaila ng gobyerno na may eleksyon sa Nobyembre.*

Exercises

a.   Answer the following questions as illustrated.

Example:
  Q: *Aling babae ang kaibigan ni Charlie?*
  A: *Ang babaeng nakapula ang kaibigan ni Charlie.*

1. *Aling doktor ang gumamot kay Jason?*
2. *Aling pulis ang umaresto kay Esperanza?*
3. *Sinong tao ang kumausap kay Wayne?*
4. *Sinong salesclerk ang hindi marunong makipag-usap?*
5. *Aling libro ang naiwala ni Preston?*

b.   Embed the sentence (B) into the host sentence (A).

	(A)	(B)
1.	*Kausapin mo ang babae.*	*Nagbabasa ng magasin ang babae.*
2.	*Hinila ang kotse.*	*Huminto ang kotse sa gitna ng daan.*
3.	*Gumawa si Miriam ng cake.*	*Paborito ni Sam ang cake.*
4.	*Bumili si Carmen ng damit sa tindahan.*	*Pinagtrabahuhan ni Sergio ang tindahan.*
5.	*Nagpabili ang Nanay ng atis.*	*Ani sa Pilipinas ang atis.*
6.	*Ikakasal si Donna kay Max.*	*Kaibigan si Max ni Jill.*
7.	*Tumikim si Ester ng pansit.*	*Niluto ni Fernando ang pansit.*

Relative Clause

Like noun complements, relative clauses also modify nouns, that is to say, they limit the range of potential referrents of the head noun. Relative clauses differ from noun complements in that the head noun serves as an argument of the verb of the embedded clause. In the example below, the head noun *tao* is subject of the verb *nanghuli.*

Hinanap ng mga pulis ang taong **nanghuli ng isda sa akwaryum.**

Study the following examples. Isolate the clause modifier. Determine the function that the head noun performs with respect to the verb of the clause.

Tinanong ni Ismael ang babaeng nakapula ng damit.
Ibinaba ng mga bumbero ang pusang nakulong sa bubong.
Hinahanap mo ba si Oscar na anak ni Mang Serafin?
Ninakaw ang librong binili ni Teddy sa Amsterdam.
Bumagsak ang mesang pinagpatungan ni Imelda ng damit.

Both relative clauses and noun complements may modify or complement a noun that serves as: subject of the host sentence, head of a non-subject non-oblique construction, head of a non-subject oblique construction, and predicate.

Modifier of Subject Nouns
Ipinagkaila ni Ramon ang bagay na **nanalo siya sa Loto Canada.**
Pinaniwalaan ni Dan ang sabi-sabi na **nasa L.A. and kaligtasan.**
Nawala ang kuwintas na **binili ni Estelita sa Honolulu.**
Niluto ni Ursula ang isdang **nabili niya sa open market.**

Modifier of Non-Subject Non-Oblique Nouns
Ginising si Renato ng balitang **bumagsak ang gobyerno ni Clark.**
Ginalit ang mga tao ng pangyayaring **hindi sumipot ang senador
    sa miting.**
Pinasaya si Domingo ng mga papuring **naririnig niya.**
Ginutom si Joaquin ng mga taong **kumidnap sa kanya.**

Modifier of Non-Subject Oblique Nouns
Ibigay mo nga ito sa taong **nakaupo sa tabi ng bintana.**
Dalhin mo ang mga gulay kay Miss Reyes na **titser ni Renato.**
Tumutol si Alfred sa mungkahing **kanselin na ang palabas.**
Sumang-ayon si John sa proposisyon na **magpadala ng delegasyon
    sa Malakanyang.**

Modifier of Predicate Nouns
*Ang balita na **uuwi si Dexter sa summer** ang nagpasaya sa Tatay.*
*Ang tanong na **hindi nasagot ni Manny** ang bumagabag sa kanya.*
*Ang taong **nakatayo sa tabi ng pinto** ang kontak ng espiya.*
*Ang abogadong **magandang magsalita** ang bagong komisyoner.*

The source of a clause modification, whether as a relative clause or a noun complement, is virtually any sentence type. Consider these sentence types:

Tumakas ang tao. (verb has one argument)
Nagdala ang tao ng mabuting balita. (verb with two arguments)
Pagod ang tao. (adjective predicate has no affix)
Masidhi ang tao. (adjective predicate has an affix)
Nasa silong and tao. (locative predicate)
Tagatalop ng patatas ang tao. (predicate is a *taga-* word)
Nakapangtrabaho ang tao. (predicate is a *naka-* word)
May tama sa balikat ang tao. (existential sentence)
Bilanggo ang tao. (predicate is a noun)

These sentences can be embedded in the host sentence *Natulog ang tao.* The head word is *tao*, which has the same referent as the noun *tao* in the lower clause, hence the second occurrence of *tao* is deleted.

Natulog ang taong tumakas (ang tao).
Natulog ang taong nagdala ng mabuting balita (ang tao).
Natulog ang taong pagod (ang tao).
Natulog ang taong masidhi (ang tao).
Natulog ang taong tagatalop ng patatas (ang tao).
Natulog ang taong nakapangtrabaho (ang tao).
Natulog ang taong may tama sa balikat (ang tao).
Natulog ang taong bilanggo (ang tao).

When the remnant of the reduced clause is a single word or a short phrase, it may be moved to precede the verb, thus, *Natulog ang pagod na tao.* This looks very much like a simple sentence whose noun subject has an adjective modifier. Might any basic sentence with a modifier have a complex sentence source after all?

Exercises

a. Combine the following sentences into one sentence. Give at least
   three combinations.

Example:
   Q: *Maliksi ang sundalo.*
       Nakailag ang sundalo.
       Sinalubong ni George ang sundalo.
   A: *Sinalubong ni George ang nakailag na sundalong maliksi.*
       Sinalubong ni George ang maliksing sundalong nakailag.
       Sinalubong ni George ang nakailag na maliksing sundalo.

1. *Binaril ng pulis ang magnanakaw.*
   Matapang ang pulis.
   Tumatakbo ang magnanakaw.

2. *Hindi nag-aral ang estudyante.*
   Naka-perm ng buhok ang estudyante.
   Kaya tutulungan mo ang estudyante.

3. *Umasenso si Gaspar.*
   Mabagal ang asenso ni Gaspar.
   Kaibigan ng Ate si Gaspar.

4. *Tahimik si Fred.*
   Magandang makisama si Fred.
   Bukas ang palad ni Fred.

5. *Ipasok mo ang balutan.*
   Dala-dala ni Jasmine ang balutan.
   Anak si Jasmine ng kaibigan ng Tatay.

b. Replace the slashes with appropriate words, phrases, or clauses.

Example:
   Q: *// tinamaan si Danil sa dibdib at /.*
   A: *Biglang tinamaan si Daniel sa dibdib at napaupo siya.*

1. *Lumakad si John ///.*

2. */ tinangay ng / agos si Derek, kay /.*

3. *Dumalaw ang babaeng /, kaya / masaya ang kuya.*

Questions with Complex Structures

Questions may have simple or complex structures depending on the noun phrase in question. Questions that focus on the actor or the patient (object) have a complex structure. The question word is predicated upon the subject, and the subject is an embedded clause.

Predicate	Subject
Sino	*ang bumili ng motorsiklo?*
Ano	*ang binili ni David?*

In contrast, questions based on location, time, and benefactor phrases are in themselves simple sentences:

Simple S:	*Bumili si David ng motorsiklo **sa Ala Moana**.*
Question:	***Saan** bumili si David ng motorsiklo?*
Simple S:	*Bumili si David ng motorsiklo **kahapon**.*
Question:	***Kailan** bumili si David ng motorsiklo?*
Simple S:	*Bumili si David ng motorsiklo **para kay Nora**.*
Question:	***Para kangino** bumili si David ng motorsiklo?*

Putting these phrases in question merely requires replacing the noun with the appropriate question word and moving the question word to the beginning of the sentence. This strategy results in incorrect questions when applied to actor and patient nouns:

Simple S:	*Bumili si David ng motorsiklo.*
Questions:	***Sino** bumili ng motorsiklo?*
	***Ano** bumili si David?*
	***Ano** binili ni David?*

Appropriate answers to complex questions have the same complex structure.

Predicate	Subject
Si David	*ang bumili ng motorsiklo.*
Motorsiklo	*ang binili ni David.*

Or the following more explicit responses:

Predicate	Subject
Si David	ang **taong** bumili ng motorsiklo.
Motorsiklo	ang **bagay** na binili ni David.

The last examples show that the subject phrase of a question that focuses on the patient or the actor consists of a head noun followed by a clause modifier, where the head noun is typically deleted.

Exercises

a. Form questions that focus on the phrases in bold.

1. *Kinabahang bigla **si Norma**.*

2. *Naglakad sa ulan **ang kaawa-awang lalaki**.*

3. *Nginitian ni Jasmine **ang trabahador**.*

4. *Ginulat si Julia **ng malakas na kulog**.*

5. *Tumanggi **siya** sa alok ni Viktor.*

6. *Pinabuksan **ito** ng lalaki sa kanya.*

7. *Iniyakan ni Teddy **ang kanyang aso**.*

8. *Pinasalamatan ni Divina **ang tumulong sa kanya**.*

9. *Ang bumunot ng ngipin ni Gilda **ang dentista**.*

10. ***Ang humihingi ng tulong** ang makakatanggap ng tulong.*

b. Form questions that focus on the nouns in bold face.

*Inihulog ni **Roberta** ang **sulat** sa **botika kahapon** para kay **Faye**.*

1.

2.

3.

4.

5.

Negatives with Complex Structures

Like questions, negative sentences that focus on the actor or the object phrase have a complex structure.

Predicate	Subject
Hindi si David	ang bumili ng motorsiklo.
Hindi motorsiklo	ang binili ni David.

Similarly with questions, negatives based on location, time, and benefactor phrases are in themselves simple sentences:

Simple S:	Bumili si David ng motorsiklo **sa Ala Moana.**
Negative:	**Hindi sa Ala Moana** bumili si David ng motorsiklo.

Simple S:	Bumili si David ng motorsiklo **kahapon.**
Negative:	**Hindi kahapon** bumili si David ng motorsiklo.

Simple S:	Bumili si David ng motorsiklo **para kay Nora.**
Negative:	**Hindi para kay Nora** bumili si David ng motorsiklo.

Negating these phrases merely requires attaching the negative particle *hindi* to the noun phrase and moving the whole phrase to the beginning of the sentence. This strategy results in incorrect questions when applied to actor and patient nouns:

Simple S:	Bumili si David ng motorsiklo.
Negatives:	***Hindi si David** bumili ng motorsiklo.
	*Hindi motorsiklo bumili si David.
	*Hindi motorsiklo binili ni David.

While the actor and object phrases can only have complex negatives, other noun phrases can have complex negatives if they can be put into focus. This holds true for questions.

Sentence:	Bumili si David ng motorsiklo para kay Nora.
Benefactor in Focus:	**Si Nora** ang ibinili ni David ng motorsiklo.
Negative:	**Hindi si Nora** ang ibinili ni David ng motorsiklo.
Question:	**Sino** ang ibinili ni David ng motorsiklo?

Sentence:	*Bumili si David ng motorsiklo sa Amerikano.*
Source	
in Focus:	**Amerikano** *ang binilhan ni David ng motorsiklo.*
Negative:	**Hindi Amerikano** *ang binilhan ni David ng motorsiklo.*
Question:	**Sino** *ang binilhan ni David ng motorsiklo?*

Time and non-personal location phrases when put in focus result in very awkward sentences.

Exercises

a. Form negatives that focus on the phrases in bold.

1. *Kinabahang bigla* **si Norma**.
2. *Naglakad sa ulan* **ang kaawa-awang lalaki**.
3. *Nginitian ni Jasmine* **ang trabahador**.
4. *Ginulat si Julia* **ng malakas na kulog**.
5. *Tumanggi* **siya** *sa alok ni Viktor*.
6. *Pinabuksan* **ito** *ng lalaki sa kanya*.
7. *Iniyakan ni Teddy* **ang kanyang aso**.
8. *Pinasalamatan ni Divina* **ang tumulong sa kanya**.
9. *Ang bumunot ng ngipin ni Gilda* **ang dentista**.
10. **Ang humihingi ng tulong** *ang makakatanggap ng tulong*.

b. Form negatives that focus on the nouns in bold face.

Inihulog ni **Roberta** *ang* **sulat** *sa* **botika kahapon** *para kay* **Faye**.

1.
2.
3.
4.
5.